unlock your
potential

Coach yourself to a life you love, and discover the
secrets of success in career and relationships

unlock your
potential

liz wilde

illustrations by
christine.wong@pvuk.com

RYLAND
PETERS
& SMALL
LONDON NEW YORK

Designers Pamela Daniels and Fiona Tweedie

Senior Editor Clare Double

Production Deborah Wehner

Art Director Gabriella Le Grazie

Publishing Director Alison Starling

Editorial Consultant Christina Rodenbeck

First published in the United States in 2004
by Ryland Peters & Small, Inc.
519 Broadway
Fifth Floor
New York NY 10012
www.rylandpeters.com

10 9 8 7 6 5 4 3 2 1

Printed in China

Library of Congress Cataloging-in-Publication Data

Wilde, Liz.
    Unlock your potential : coach yourself to a life you love, and discover the secrets of
success in career and relationships / Liz Wilde.

        p. cm.
    ISBN 1-84172-592-7
  1. Self-actualization (Psychology) 2. Success--Psychological aspects.
3. Self-help techniques. 4. Self-talk. I. Title.
    BF637.S4W488 2004
    158.1--dc22

                                                    2003020617

contents

In this book you will see symbols. These denote information or exercises, as follows:

your way forward

what's in your way

pick one of these

> We either make ourselves miserable or we make
> ourselves strong. The amount of work is the same.
>
> CARLOS CASTANEDA (1925 – 1998)

While none of my clients is ever the same, the majority come to me looking for an answer to the following questions. Is this it? Is this the best life can be? Surely there's a better way? Their dissatisfaction with life may be vague or all-consuming, but one thing is certain. They're not sure how they got *here*, and they certainly don't know how to get *there*.

introduction: is this it?

The first step is to find out what my clients really want their lives to look like. "What do you really, really want?" can be the most frightening question a life coach can ask. "That's the problem, I don't know!" is a common response, but this is often little more than an excuse—even if the client doesn't realize it yet. It can be very scary letting yourself think about what you want in life, especially if it's not what you have.

People are often unable to take the first step because they're terrified of what will happen once they start. Fear can keep you stuck forever. Fear of failure, fear of the past repeating itself, fear of being rejected, fear of being exposed as a fraud. But we get back from life what we expect, so if you believe you won't succeed, chances are no one's going to argue with you. Who you are determines how well you do things, and you need to be strong enough on the inside to take effective action. We all have natural qualities and talents—only you can decide when you're ready to develop your own.

Your inner thoughts determine everything you do. What you believe you're capable of is exactly what you'll achieve. Everyone I've coached has a story that keeps them stuck. What they believe about themselves has helped create the life they have now. These beliefs begin in childhood and expand into something like this:

"I'm not clever enough to get a degree like the rest of my family."

"I'm far too disorganized to start my own business."

"We've all got a sweet tooth in my family so I'll always be overweight."

"I'm useless with money so no wonder I'm always broke."

Unfortunately, the negative messages we receive throughout life far outnumber the positive, so it's no surprise the majority of our self-beliefs end up seriously limiting our possibilities.

People can be unaware of how they've created what's happened in their lives so far. They blame their genes, circumstances, parents—in fact, anything but themselves —for blocking their potential. But the truth is, no one has ever caused your life to be one way or another. It's been your choice all along. Make a list of everything that's happened in your adult life and you can start to see how you've helped to create it. The most important thing I can do is help you see that you have a choice in what you think; that at any moment you're choosing the way you feel. And if that thought is sabotaging you, you can drop it and choose another. This can only happen when someone starts to live consciously. Until then, they make unconscious decisions based on what their mother/boss/friends/partner thinks they *should* be doing.

Living consciously means looking at your behavior and seeing how it's gotten you to where you are today. If who you are and what you have right now is the result of your thoughts, and you don't change them, your future will look exactly the same. It can be very hard to admit you've been your own worst enemy, and to see how many times you've sabotaged your own happiness or gotten in the way of your own success. But awareness is your way out. Once you see how you've helped create your own dissatisfaction, you can start to see how you can create your own happiness—and live a life you love.

I want you to use me as your life coach and this book as our sessions together. A life coach is a little like an athlete's sports coach, but instead of achieving better levels of fitness and performance, we will work towards improving your quality of life significantly. Successful coaching demands courage and commitment. The more honest you are, the more you'll get out of this book, so please take your time over the exercises. Very soon you'll start to see that changing the way you think will change the way you live your life forever. If you want to live your potential, this book is for you.

part 1

What would make you *really* happy?

Happiness is the world's most
enviable commodity, yet it's far easier
to achieve than status or wealth.
And there's enough for everyone.

finding your passions

Discovering what really matters to you is the first step toward living your potential. No matter what you may think, life doesn't have to be difficult. Do the things that are really *you* and life works so much better. Your passions are things that you're naturally drawn towards and you do well—often with little effort. They *are* you. And when you live a life that's designed around your passions, you cannot help feeling fulfilled. RESULT: An inner happiness and satisfaction which comes from the knowledge that you're being totally true to yourself. From your passions, comes the life you've always dreamed of.

What gets in the way of you **living your passions?**

Lack of awareness

Fear

Saying yes when what you really mean is no

Being too busy

Waiting for something to happen

Playing the victim

Living in the past or the future

Low self-esteem

Shoulds and supposed tos

Not taking responsibility for your life

Stress

Living a lifestyle versus a life

Limiting beliefs

Putting yourself second (or last)

Acting out of habit

Low expectations

Not realizing it's possible to live the life you want

What do you **love** to do?

When did you last feel really passionate about something?

Think back to when you were last really happy. What were you doing? Exactly what was it about the situation that made you feel so good? Read the following questions and pick out the words in *italics* that feel really important to you. Remember, if you've felt like this since you were young, this is a true passion.

Do you love to *learn* new things?
Or do you prefer passing your knowledge on by *teaching* others?

Is life an *adventure* or nothing at all?
Or do you prefer to feel *safe* and *nurtured* as part of a community?

Do you feel most alive when you're *laughing* and *having fun*?
Or when you *accomplish* a goal? (Or even score one!)

Are *beautiful* surroundings really important to you?
Or is it more important to feel deeply *connected* with those around you?

Are you happiest being totally *uncommitted*?
Or do you feel most fulfilled showing *love* and *compassion* to others?

Do you thrive on being an *expert* in your field?
Do you love to *inspire* and *influence* others?
Or do you get more satisfaction offering *support* to those in need?

Are you uncomfortable if you're not being totally *authentic*?
Are you stifled if you're not *creating* something?

Do you feel happiest being *part of a team* or a *leader*?
Or do you prefer to be totally *independent*?

1 Make a list

of the words that really struck you (and any others not included on the list that came into your head as you read it). Now, choose the five that feel the most important— these are your most powerful passions.

2 Commit

to taking one action to support each of your five passions in the next 28 days.

Live as you like best and your character will take care of itself.

HENRY JAMES (1843–1916)

If you love to learn, book a course in something you've always been interested in, or read something that stretches your mind every day.

If you love adventure, plan a trip to somewhere you've never been before or join a mountaineering/skydiving/cycling club.

If you love beautiful things, remove everything ugly from your living space and replace at least one item with a far more attractive alternative.

If you love to feel connected, arrange a weekly family get-together or a regular night out with your closest friends.

If you love to create, enroll in an art evening class or redecorate your home.

If you love to support others, offer your help to a charitable organization or a friend in need.

Help—I don't feel passionate about anything!

When life is one big to-do list, you can easily forget what was once important to you. You will never get what you want if you don't know what that is, so your first step is to slow down and take time to rediscover your passions. Switch off the TV for a month, leave work at 5:30 every night and spend time by yourself. Start to notice what you think about and what you enjoy. Try lots of new things (a cooking class, hot yoga, life drawing, salsa dancing) and listen to what your body and mind tell you. Most of us are desperate to find out what will make us happy, but never really bother to look. You need to get out there and explore life's opportunities, because one thing's for sure, they won't find you while you're sitting on the sofa every night watching other people's lives on TV.

When you're living your life in harmony with your passions, you'll feel more fulfilled than you ever thought possible. Guaranteed. And that's just the beginning.

Reasons to **design your life** around your passions

1 **It gives you pleasure.** Everything that brings you joy comes from your passions.

2 **It lets you be true to yourself.** When you know what you love to do, you can do more of it (and less of the other stuff).

3 **It allows you to give up goals that weren't really yours** in the first place. Once you see what you were meant to do, you can understand why some goals you've had for years just haven't happened. That's because they were goals based on someone else's agenda, rather than goals that support your passions. Give them up and watch the guilt disappear.

4 **It makes decisions much easier.** Next time you're faced with a decision, put it up against your passions. Which option supports what is important to you? A job abroad may sound glamorous, but if feeling safe and nurtured by a close community makes you happy, living halfway around the world will not, no matter how impressive the salary.

5 **It makes goal-setting much easier, too.** Now that you know what you love to do, you can set goals that support your passions. Do it this way and rather than struggle, you'll feel a natural pull in the right direction.

6 **It makes sense of your behavior** around certain people or in some situations. Ever wondered why someone can irritate you beyond belief, yet get on fine with your friends? Or how you feel suffocated in certain situations? That's because something or someone is threatening the very things that are most important to you and you feel the need to defend yourself.

7 **It helps you choose better environments.** Now you can actively seek out the people and places that support you, knowing why they make you feel good.

8 **It gives you far more energy.** Living a life designed around what really matters to you creates a natural energy that makes everything feel so much easier. Try it and see.

Loving what you do for a living

If you work at something you love, you will not only be happier, you'll also be far more likely to succeed—and even make more money! The world's most successful people have chosen careers they naturally enjoy. So ask yourself: What would my passions lead me to do for a living? How can I alter my present job to include some of my passions? If I woke up a year from now and had my dream job, what would it look like? What can I do this week to begin moving me closer toward this perfect career?

FACT: When you're passionate about what you do, you will never again have to drag yourself out of bed in the morning.

But it's impossible!

The idea of designing your life around what's really important to you may seem a distant dream, but nothing's impossible. It may just be a bit inconvenient for a while.

ASK YOURSELF: What am I willing to do to live my dream? Going back to college to study homeopathy may mean you have to take an evening job, stop buying new clothes for a year, and even rent out your spare room, but none of these things is life-threatening. What's far more destructive is staying in a job you hate while dreaming of what life would be like if you'd taken the plunge and retrained as a homeopath.

DO YOU HAVE A LIFE OR A LIFESTYLE?

Why are you doing a job if you're not enjoying it? For the money, of course! For the lifestyle it buys you. So what does this job give you? A shiny new car, an exotic foreign holiday, the latest designer clothes? And what does it cost you? Stress, frustration, exhaustion? Only you can decide if the price is too high.

the power of pleasure

Do you have trouble getting up in the morning? Have you ever mentally skipped through the day and not found a single thing worth the effort of getting vertical? Then it's about time you took control of your life and started setting up what you want to happen each day.

When was the last time you let yourself have a little fun? Chances are no one has ever told you to get more pleasure in your life. Study harder, perhaps. Work harder, almost definitely. But play harder? Not likely.

How do I get **more pleasure?**

Easy. All you have to do is *choose* to do things that make you feel good. Pleasure is a choice just as hard work is a choice. And unhappiness. But most of us need permission to adopt such a hedonistic frame of mind. We would much rather struggle through life exhausted by the constant chores we really *should* do, rather than energized by the feel-good stuff we *could* do.

Pleasure is the secret to a happy life, yet giving yourself permission to grab it at every opportunity is a skill most of us lost at school. From an early age, we were taught that hard work is the (nonrefundable) ticket to a successful existence. We were told to ignore our desires and settle down to the serious business of getting through life. But don't feel resentful for all those years of missed fun and pleasure —your teachers and parents were only passing on what they'd been taught themselves. Who can blame them for wanting you to follow in their footsteps? They had the evidence. Life was tough and the only reason they had what they had today was through hard labor. If they'd given up precious time for pleasure, goodness knows what would have become of them!

Pleasing yourself is the only guaranteed way you will experience pure happiness, because if you wait for others to give you pleasure, you're not only giving up your power, you'll probably be waiting a very long time, too.

Make a list of 10 daily pleasures that would bring you joy.

Not things that you should do, but things that you'll look forward to and really enjoy (but would usually forget to do in a day which is otherwise filled with tasks and chores).

What would you enjoy every day?

A freshly squeezed fruit juice in the morning

A glass of red wine at night

Wearing silk underwear

Wearing cashmere pajamas

A walk in the park at lunchtime

A yoga class in the evening

Talking to a friend who makes you laugh

Hugging someone you love

A mid-morning cappuccino

A mid-afternoon meditation

Playing your favorite music

Watching your favorite TV show

Reading a good book

Reading a trashy gossip magazine

And don't forget those treats you wouldn't normally allow yourself because they feel far too indulgent—that's the point! Think of things like an hour-long soak in the bath, a glass of champagne, a manicure, an afternoon nap—and include at least one a week.

No one has ever looked back and regretted being so nice to themselves. And if it's good for you, chances are it's going to benefit everyone else around you, too. So the next time you feel less than happy, ask yourself this question: "What is the one thing I can do right now that will bring me joy?" Then give yourself permission to do it. Not tomorrow, not at the weekend, but right now.

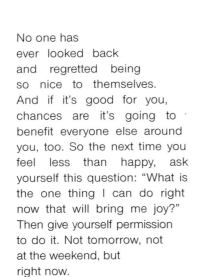

Rediscover **your funnybone**

Life is serious enough without you taking yourself too seriously.
A fact that may surprise you: most of us are about as happy as we
decide to be. The same bad day at the office can send one worker
home determined to have a good evening (the day's been bad
enough, why make it worse?), while their coworker may dwell on
the day's events for a week. The result? The second worker gains
nothing from suffering for seven days, except perhaps a future ulcer.
The first worker may watch a comedy show or talk to a friend who
makes them laugh. And suddenly they no longer feel bad, because
it's impossible to feel bad when you're laughing.

WHY IS LAUGHTER GOOD FOR YOU?

Laughing is like taking your lungs to the gym. When you have a good
belly laugh, endorphins associated with exercise are released in your
brain. This sets off all kinds of internal fireworks, resulting in a feel-
fantastic natural high. No copious amounts of alcohol required.

It's long been said that laughter is the best medicine, and
no wonder. Laughing activates natural "killer" cells that help fight
infection and disease. It also speeds up the production of new
immune cells and reduces levels of the stress hormone, cortisol.
And laughter is life's natural painkiller. A good laugh is guaranteed
to relax even the tensest body, and the more relaxed you are, the
less pain you can feel. There's even evidence that happy people
live significantly longer than others.

There are plenty of reasons to look on the bright side, but society
doesn't see it that way. The average child laughs around 300 times a
day, compared to the meager 17 chuckles adults allow themselves.
But it's not too late to rediscover your childhood love of laughter. If
you're serious about improving your life, the first step is to stop taking
it (and yourself) so seriously.

Make a list of everything that makes you laugh.

Include things you most enjoy doing
on your own and things you enjoy
doing with one or more of your friends.

Put the list somewhere you can see
it and do your smiley stuff as often
as possible.

* Invest in a boxed set of your
  favorite funny TV show and keep
  it handy for those post-bad-day-
  at-the-office evenings.
* Visit a comedy club and leave
  with face ache.
* Get your friends around with their
  old photos. Laugh like crazy at
  your 1980s poodle perm.

Do whatever it takes to put a smile
on your face.

be your own talent scout

You are unique—just like everyone else. Only you can decide what you've got to offer the world. What are you good at? What have you been good at all your life? Now, what are you doing with all that you were given? If you're not using your talents, you can't expect life to get much better—or easier. FACT: The majority of people who are rich and successful aren't lucky, they've just found a way to make a living doing something they're good at.

Most of us are stuck in a job chosen by a sixteen-year-old—you! And what were your reasons for the choice you made? At that crucial decision time in your life, you were probably heavily influenced by your parents (either to do what they wanted you to do—or to revolt by choosing the opposite). But four years of study, followed by five to ten years of experience, doesn't have to mean another 30 years in the job. That's a life sentence, and it's doing no one any good—not your parents (who most of all want you to be happy), or you.

There's a saying, "nature doesn't kill itself," meaning, if you love to do something, chances are you're pretty good at it. And if you work at something you love, you are far more likely to succeed.

Stuck on your strengths?

We all have a blind spot when it comes to naming our strengths, but get us started on our weaknesses and we can talk for hours. There are three ways to discover your talents:

1 Ask yourself: What can I give? rather than, what can I get?

2 Ask people close to you what they think you're good at.

3 Turn it around. Think about what irritated you when you were growing up. What irritated others about you? Were you stubborn? Great, that means you won't give up if things don't go exactly according to plan. Were you always being told off for talking too much? At last you can put your natural communication skills to good use and find a job where you get to talk for a living!

NATURAL TALENTS

Having a talent doesn't mean reaching grade five on the piano or being able to draw to scale. It simply means you have a skill that comes naturally. Read the following list for inspiration.

Communicator	Creative	Patient
Diplomatic	Organized	Imaginative
Fast learner	Hard-working	**Visionary**
Excel under pressure	**Artistic**	Conscientious
Intuitive	Determined	Tolerant
Leader	**Sociable**	**Public speaker**
Quick thinker	Persuasive	Tenacious
Problem solver	Dedicated	Inventive
Multi-tasker	**Adaptable**	**Motivating**
Visual	Kind	Resilient
Optimistic	Courageous	Curious
Good listener	**Quick-witted**	Team player

The funny thing about strengths is we tend to think far more about other people's than about our own. Chances are you hold your sister's university degree in higher esteem than your successful job in advertising. We all underestimate what we can do compared to our family, friends, and coworkers, but fulfillment comes from recognizing your own talents and putting them to good use, not wishing you were more academic like your sister.

Ask yourself: what's distinctive about me?

Write a list of your top ten talents, beginning each sentence: "I am good at … "

Now, what can you do to put these to good use?
What talents are you currently not making the most of?
How can you change your job to fully use each one of your talents?
What new career could you choose to utilize the skills that come naturally to you?
What talent would it feel great to focus your life around?

step four

discover your needs

Now that you know what you want, the next step is to find out what you need. The difference? You may want to make a million, but you need $1,000 in the bank to feel safe and secure. Don't underestimate your needs. Knowing what they are is essential for you to live your best life, as needs seriously drain your energy unless you find a way to get them satisfied. Usually needs come from a lack in your life when you were growing up. Perhaps your parents weren't affectionate. Not because they didn't love you, but because showing affection simply wasn't important to them. You've grown up into an adult who needs affection to feel good about yourself. The less affection you receive, the more needy you become. Fortunately, you're now in a position to take responsibility for fulfilling this need yourself. But you didn't create the need on your own, so there's no reason why you have to do all the work to get it satisfied. There are two ways to get a need satisfied: do it for yourself or ask those close to you to do it for you. But first you have to discover what needs you have that must be met for you to be happy and fulfilled.

Identify your needs

Choose the needs that mean most to you from the list on the right (and any others not included that come into your head as you read it). Don't rush. You may not even be aware that you need something because you've become so clever at hiding it from others and yourself. ASK YOURSELF: When was the last time you flew into a rage? What part of you was threatened that caused such an extreme reaction? What need was ignored or under attack? Now choose your top five needs and commit to getting them satisfied. You'll be much happier for it.

What do you need in order to be happy?

To speak (and hear) the truth

Safety and security

Peace and quiet

Appreciation

Praise

Respect

Acceptance

Affection

Lots of space

To feel really listened to

Attention

To feel protected

Savings in the bank

Total **loyalty**

To feel needed

To be included

Time alone

To be authentic

To give (and receive) commitment

Freedom

Encouragement

Trust

To feel you **belong**

Get your needs satisfied

Supposing your need is to receive affection. How can you get this satisfied so that you feel good inside?

1 **You can begin by showing yourself affection.** Unless you handle your own need for affection, no amount from others will ever be enough.

❊ Buy flowers for your home.

❊ Treat yourself to your favorite foods.

❊ Have a weekly massage.

❊ Put yourself first.

❊ Only wear clothes that make you feel great.

❊ Sleep on 100% Egyptian cotton bed linen.

❊ Burn essential oils in your bedroom.

❊ Be kinder to yourself when you make a mistake.

❊ Do something you really enjoy every day.

❊ Make a decision never to criticize yourself again.

2 **You can ask others directly for what you want** using an "I" statement to explain exactly what your need is.

❊ ASK YOUR PARTNER: I need to receive affection.

Will you kiss me every night when you come home from work?

❊ ASK YOUR FRIENDS: I really love affection.

Will you hug me every time we meet up?

❊ ASK YOUR FAMILY: Affection is very important to me.

Will you regularly show me how much I mean to you?

3 **You can also ask to hear the exact words** that will satisfy your need. By listening to the actual statement you need to hear, your brain will accept it and be satisfied. Supposing you need to feel appreciated. Choose three people close to you and tell them what you need to hear: I need to feel appreciated. Will you regularly tell me that you appreciate me? Remember, no one person can satisfy all your needs, so set up a committee to do the job. And if anyone resists, simply choose another committee member.

step five

what can you do today?

Now that you know the things you want and need in order to be happy, ask yourself this question: What's the one thing I can do today that will begin to improve my life? What's the one change I can make in my life today that will result in the biggest difference? Most of us get overwhelmed at the thought of change and end up doing absolutely nothing, but as Abraham Lincoln said:

The best thing about the future is that it comes only one day at a time. It's your choice if you decide to use each day 100 percent.

part 2

What's holding you back?

Most of us are our worst enemy. Would you
dream of judging your friends so harshly?

step one

where are you
sabotaging yourself?

Who do you think you are? Your thoughts about yourself determine everything you do. Yet most of your basic beliefs are formed back in childhood. The totally dependent toddler who was unable to think logically, decided how you were going to see and feel about yourself 10, 20, 30 years into the future, and these beliefs now completely create your reality.

By the time you reach ten years old, you'll have experienced significantly more negative messages about yourself, compared to positive ones. No wonder the majority of us are now the not-so-proud owners of a less than positive self-image. Add constant media pressure to be perfect (model-thin, celebrity-sexy, athletic-fit, mogul-rich), and most of us are left feeling very inadequate.

The good news is you're now fully grown and able to make a more accurate assessment based on adult logic. We all have a choice about what we think— what if you were to choose a new belief that supports rather than sabotages you? If you want to change any area of your life, you first have to change your mind around it. Remember, who you are and what you have in your life right now is the result of your thoughts. Unless you change your thoughts, your future will look exactly the same as your present.

You have many beliefs about yourself (some good, some not so good), and awareness of them is the first step toward changing the ones that limit you. We're often not even aware that a belief is seriously getting in the way of our happiness because it's so deeply ingrained, it feels a part of who we are.

Beliefs that block you

I'm not smart/attractive/good enough.

It's my fault if other people are angry/upset/disappointed.

I cannot trust my own decisions.

It's unforgivable to make a mistake.

I'm a victim of my past/circumstances/genes.

It's too pushy/rude to ask for what I want.

I'm selfish if I put myself first.

I'm not worthy of other people's time/love/respect.

It's arrogant/egotistical to love myself.

A belief is just a thought you keep thinking. You can break the vicious cycle by recognizing what's behind a thought and choosing a different one that makes you feel good about yourself. If you don't like something about yourself, remember it's just a belief. Isn't it time you chose a better one?

One's own thought is one's world.
What a person thinks is what he becomes.

THE UPANISHADS (7TH CENTURY B.C.)

Busting an old belief, step by step:

1 **Start to notice how you behave,** especially in stressful and unhappy situations. What are you thinking about yourself? Do you notice a pattern? ASK YOURSELF: What belief am I holding onto in order for me to be feeling this way?

> FEELING: I'm frightened of making a mistake.
> BELIEF: I must be competent in everything I do
> or I'm a failure.

> FEELING: I'll never be happy.
> BELIEF: The past will repeat itself and I've no
> control over my future.

> FEELING: I can only wear designer clothes.
> BELIEF: I'm not a success unless other people
> see how much I can afford to spend.

> FEELING: I'm unable to say no.
> BELIEF: If I don't please people they will dislike me.

2 **Is this belief really true?** Does one mistake really make you a failure? Do you really have to be a doormat in order to be liked? Why do you believe this?

3 **How would your life improve** if you chose a different belief to replace this old one? Can you see any good in sticking with this outdated belief about yourself or the world?

4 **Enough with the self-criticism.** Is there a different way to look at this situation? One that feels a whole lot better? Choose a new belief today that supports you and watch your behavior change.

I do the best I can and nothing else matters.

I can learn from the past to create a better future.

I'm proud of my life, not my lifestyle.

Pleasing myself is the only way I can please others.

As you continue to think your new thought, notice how previously stressful situations no longer have the power to hurt you.

Label **conscious**

Beware. When you believe something about yourself it can become a self-fulfilling prophecy.
Labels stick. Recognize yourself?

"I'm a procrastinator."

This is the perfect excuse for inaction, but all it really does is stop you from doing
what could make you very happy.

Who said you were a procrastinator? Did you give yourself this

label or did it come from a teacher, friend, or parent? Is it really true? Write a list
of the times you took action and got what you wanted. Collect evidence that
when you *really* want to go after something, you do just that. And reap the
rewards! Find someone you respect (and don't want to let down) to hold you
accountable for your actions. Check in with them once a week to monitor your
progress. Or promise yourself a reward (flowers/a manicure/a bar of chocolate)
after each successfully completed action step.

"I'm a perfectionist."

This makes life very complicated, as nothing's ever quite right or good enough.
Wait around for the perfect time/job/partner and you'll never live your life to the full.
It's also a great excuse for doing nothing unless the outcome's guaranteed.

Replace perfectionism with pride. Does being a perfectionist

make you happy? Who told you everything you do has to be perfect? Does this
person still have the right to affect your life? Take the pressure off and commit to
doing something imperfect every day. Start with the small things (try ignoring
mess in your home or even wearing odd socks!), and work up to the bigger stuff.
This may mean making a few mistakes, but they shouldn't be serious.

Breaking bad habits

We all have habits that get in the way of our being our best. Often they are so much a part of us that we completely take them for granted. Call yourself lazy? Then that's what you'll be. Can't help your sweet tooth? Don't be so sure.

Habits are simply an automatic reaction to a specific situation. When you experience the trigger, you react out of habit, without thinking. But just as habits are learned, they can be relearned, too, although be prepared for a little work. You wouldn't expect to learn to play an instrument in a weekend, so don't expect changing the habit of (possibly) a lifetime to be a 48-hour job either.

You're probably unaware of how much you affect, and even cause, the things that happen in your life. But creating new habits means you can start to choose the life you want, rather than living according to some old script you picked up many years ago.

Replace an old habit with a new one, step by step:

1 **First you need to understand** what you get out of this behavior. Every habit has a positive payback, whether you're conscious of it or not. How has this habit served you in the past?
   Working long hours excuses you from admitting there's little else in your life.
   Arguing with your partner guarantees you get constant attention.
   Continuous complaining about your bad luck gets you lots of sympathy.

2 **Make clear** the reason you're going to replace this old habit with a new one. What are the benefits?

3 **Put your new habit into words** and memorize the statement word for word so you can easily recite it to yourself when your old behavior threatens.
   I finish at 5:30 and spend my evenings enjoying life.
   I believe it's more important to be happy than right.
   I'm in control of my life and choose to change what I don't like.

4 **Practice your new habit** over and over again, even when it seems easier to go back to the old one. Your new habit may feel false at first, but as you continue to practice, it'll begin to get easier.

5 **With constant practice** you'll become so comfortable with this new behavior, it'll be automatic. Congratulations! You've just created a brand new habit.

Don't go around saying the world owes you a living. The world owes you nothing. It was here first.

MARK TWAIN (1835 – 1910)

Stop expecting, **start living**

When you expect something to turn out just the way you want, you're setting yourself up for disappointment. When was the last time you:

Started sizing someone up as spouse material after only a few dates?
Worked overtime every night so your boss would give you a raise?
Thought "you owe me one" after doing a friend a favor?

You can't avoid disappointment if you count on things turning out just the way you expect them to. Especially when you take each let-down personally. What you need to understand is that no one's doing anything against you. Your date is just enjoying your company. Your boss is just pleased to be handing over some responsibility. Your friend is just grateful for your help. How can anyone know what you expect if you don't tell them? No one can read your mind. See right for a new perspective.

❋ Instead of analyzing every word your new partner says, relax and enjoy yourself.

❋ Instead of working hard to get more money, work because you enjoy it and take pride in your achievements (this may mean changing what you do!).

❋ Enjoy doing someone a favor.

AS CONFUCIUS SAYS: He who wishes to secure the good of others has already secured his own.

What areas of your life are on hold while you magically expect things to change? How often do you catch yourself thinking: If only ... would happen, I could be happy? When ... happens I will finally be happy?

 Pick one area and list five actions you can take that will get you unstuck and moving forward. Choose the easiest one and do it today. What unfulfilled expectations are you carrying around every day?

... owes me a favor!
I work hard and deserve ...
My partner should ...
Why don't my parents/friends do ...?

Do any of these people *know* this is how you feel? Nothing wastes time more than waiting for others to work out what you want. They'd be much happier if you just asked them for it.

FACT: Expectations are the number one reason why relationships fail. If you expect things to be a certain way, not only do you risk being disappointed, but life can't come in and make it better.

How to ask for what you want, step by step:

1 **Give yourself permission** to ask for what you want. Whether it's help with the housework or a raise, you have a right to ask for what you want from anyone you want it from.

2 **Don't assume** the other person should have known what you wanted in the first place. They have different priorities to you and it's your job to bring your priorities to their attention.

3 **Ask, don't demand.** Be prepared for a no, but ask well, and you're more likely to get a yes.

4 **Remember it works both ways.** Ask what you can do for the other person and give *them* what they want.

5 **If you get a yes, show your appreciation** and they'll be far more likely to say yes next time.

How often do you think: I've been let down before—why should I trust anyone again? Someone else always gets what I want, so what's the point in trying?

live out of your imagination—not your past

Letting the past predict the future is a great big excuse. It lets you believe that some version of what happened in the past can happen to you again in the future. But this can only be true if you let it. Who or what caused your pain can only have power over you if you let yourself focus on these feelings. It's much better to live in the life you have now and stop searching for a meaning in or reason for the past. Accepting the reality of what happened and not wasting time on regrets is the only way to get over the past, enjoy the present, and look forward to the future.

FACT: You will only be happy in the present if you give up hope of a better past. Forgiving others always works in your favor. The only person who suffers from holding a grudge is the person with their hands full. Most people have forgiveness worked out the wrong way around. If you believe that refusing to forgive someone is making them unhappy, you're wrong. Withholding forgiveness is your problem, not theirs. You're the one suffering the sleepless nights. They probably sleep like a log.

Refusing to forgive is a major obstacle to happiness. It's a power game and one that can only get in the way of living your best life. This kind of control may feel powerful, but the real power lies in letting go. You can only be happy now if you stop trying to change the past—something no one has ever succeeded in doing, although many of us spend a lifetime trying.

Forgiveness doesn't have to make what happened to you acceptable, and forgiving certainly doesn't mean you're open to a repeat performance. What's important is to learn from the situation so that you need never suffer in the same way again. History only repeats itself when no one listens the first time. Make sure you listen and learn.

How to put the past behind you (where it belongs)

Make a list of who you need to forgive and write down what was actually done that gave you pain. Not what you felt at the time, but the facts.

Recognize who is being hurt by your refusal to forgive. Is the other person lying awake at night burning with anger and resentment? Probably not.

We often need to know why before we allow ourselves to forgive, but sometimes there's no reason. We didn't know why when we felt the pain, so knowing now is not necessarily going to make it better.

Stop playing the victim in your story. Chances are you had some part in what happened, whether it was just hiding the fact you were hurt at the time, or staying around long after you could have left. Admitting to just some of the responsibility can go a long way toward understanding the problem—and even more importantly, making sure it never happens again

Now take a deep breath and let it go. If you need to take action, write a letter to the other person saying everything you've ever wanted to (but is probably best kept to yourself). Then hit the delete key—and get on with your life.

Playing the **blame game**

Blame gets you nowhere. While you're stuck in the blame cycle, you're
refusing to take responsibility for your own life. Only when you stop blaming others
for the stuff you don't like, will you be in a position to do something about it.

Blaming is another big bad excuse. As long as you make another person
responsible, then there's nothing you can do. But blaming others never resolved
a situation, only taking action can do that. The same goes for blaming your
circumstances. When a situation's not what we think it should be, we try to regain a
feeling of control by blaming everyone and everything around us. And as long as we
play this game, we give ourselves the illusion of control. But it's just an illusion. How
can we possibly control something that's already happened? Much easier to take
control of the present, because you really *can* do something about that.

Blitz your blame list

Who or what is on your blame list? Your mother, for not encouraging you to follow your
dreams? Your school guidance counsellor, for not explaining all the options? Your
father, for insisting you go to university while all your friends took a year out first?

Well, you're in luck. As a fully grown up human being, you can now make all your
own choices. You can choose to go after your dream job now. You can choose to
take a year out now. You can choose to do anything that makes you happy. But you
can't make this choice while you're still stuck on blaming others. At last, the choice
is yours to make. Doesn't that feel good?

Forgiving yourself

Many people spend their whole lives punishing themselves for past real or imagined deeds. "If only you knew the *terrible* things I've done!," they say (to themselves). So they eat too much or too little, drink until they can't think, and push away anyone who's stupid enough to love them. Don't they *know*? All because they don't love themselves enough. A FACT OF LIFE: If you believe you don't deserve the best, no one is going to argue with you.

Taking good care of yourself is a sign that you value what you are and what you've got. But some people take more care of their car or cashmere sweater than they do of their bodies. Otherwise they'd want to eat things that give them lots of energy (not leave them tired and bloated). And they'd want to do exercise that de-stresses their mind (not makes them feel guilty—unused gym membership anyone?). Only when you forgive yourself will you want to put just the right amount of healthy food in your mouth. Because you know t makes you look and feel good. And you *deserve* to look and feel good. And only when you forgive yourself will you not want to "medicate" the outside world, because you actually quite like it.

Giving yourself the gift of forgiveness is just about the most powerful present money can't buy. It'll not only change the way you think about yourself, it'll change the way you look after yourself, too. And it really is easier than you think.

FINDING WAYS TO FORGIVE YOURSELF

How long are you prepared to feel bad about what you've done? Another year or two, or a whole lifetime? That's your choice, but before you make yourself miserable for the rest of your days, consider this. Is your suffering actually helping the person you feel you've wronged so badly? Probably not, in which case, why prolong the agony? Far better to learn from your mistakes and realize you did the best you could with what you had then. Guilty feelings now simply mean your standards are much higher. A cause for celebration, not regret.

 step three

Do you ever feel you've so much going on you can't make a decision about anything? Human beings can only ever hold six thoughts in their heads at any one time. Try to cram in more and our brains become overwhelmed, leaving us incapable of even the simplest choice.

why we **stay stuck**

10 early warning signs that you're a busyholic

You keep losing your keys.

You don't have time to return calls to friends.

You haven't read your book for so long you have to go back to the beginning.

All your self-care rituals have gone out of the window.

Your space is overflowing with clutter.

You feel you're on a speeding train and want to get off.

Your memory is like a sieve.

You rarely taste what you're eating.

Your day is spent on crisis management.

You create more work for yourself by rushing everything in front of you.

How to kick the busy habit. What you say—and the questions to ask yourself:

"I've no time." How much time this week have you spent on activities that have no meaning to you? Aren't you more important?

"My to-do list is too long already." How can you look at the big picture if you're continuously working through the details of the day? What's really important to accomplish in the long term?

"I'm so cluttered I can't think straight." Are you using chaos to distract you from paying attention to what you really want to do? How can you clear some space so that you have time to spend on yourself?

"My schedule is full." Why have you convinced yourself that every second of your life has to be planned out? Do all these activities still make sense? What can you drop that no longer fits into your life?

"I have to do everything myself." Is that really true? Who do you have in your life that you could delegate to? Why are you afraid of letting go of control? What's the worst that can happen?
CLUE: The job or task may not be quite up to your standards.

"I feel guilty doing nothing." Who told you that relaxing was the same as collapsing? Why do you believe you don't deserve time to recharge your batteries?

Are you addicted to adrenaline?
You're always late.

You put work off and then have to rush it.

You feel constantly under pressure.

You shout at other drivers.

You demand an immediate response.

You have no patience with others.

You speak very fast.

You can't relax.

You miss the buzz when there's no pressure to perform.

The definition of crazy is doing the same thing again and expecting a different outcome. Yet most of us spend our lives doing exactly the same thing and hoping that somehow it will work out right this time. Think of a situation that isn't working for you. What are you doing to resolve it, and how long have you been doing this same thing? What will happen if you continue to do the same thing for the next five years? Now get creative. What is life telling you to do differently? You can't solve a problem with the same thought that created it. What one thing could you do differently today to get you unstuck and moving forward?

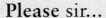

I have been though some terrible things in my life, some of which actually happened.

MARK TWAIN (1835–1910)

Please sir...

Whose permission do you need before you take action? Maybe when you were growing up you had to ask your parents/teachers/siblings/friends before doing just about anything, but as an adult you don't have to ask anyone ever again.

Write yourself out a permission form:

I give myself permission to ... do whatever I want!

Now, what are you waiting for?

Your own **worst enemy?**

The terrible things you say to yourself are seriously getting in the way of your living a successful life. Would you ever talk to another person the way you talk to yourself? Negative self-talk is a major energy drain that wears you down. And while you're beating yourself up, it's almost impossible to change your life for the better.

Count the number of times you indulge in negative self-talk. Become conscious of the things you say to yourself, and start to put them under investigation. Are they really accurate? Would you judge your friends and family so harshly?

Indulge in a little positive pampering

1   Make a list of all the times you've set out to do
    something and succeeded.

2   Write down all the things that are going right, right now.

One major reason why people fail? They feel like they've
never succeeded, so they don't believe they ever can.
Pin your list on the fridge door and read it every day to
remind yourself just how successful you really are.

What are you **waiting for?**

It can seem easier to wait for a decision to be taken out
of your hands, but while you're wishing something (or
someone) would happen, other people are getting on with
their lives. A WORD OF WARNING: Those who wait usually get
what no one else wants. Playing the waiting game actually
pushes your power to change things onto something or
someone else, giving you no control. And don't hold your
breath. Ever noticed how a watched phone never rings?

Where in your life are you waiting for something to
happen? While you're waiting to be discovered as the next
big thing, do what it takes to improve the life you have right
now. You may just find that when that talent scout comes
knocking, you really don't need their help any more.

part 3

What are you
afraid of?

There are really only two emotions—love and fear.
When you're feeling jealous, upset, disappointed,
or angry, what you're really feeling is scared.
And when you're stuck, you're plain terrified.

Courage is resistance to fear, mastery
of fear. Not the absence of fear.

MARK TWAIN (1835 – 1910)

escape your comfort zone

Our instinct for security is often greater than our instinct for success,
and the status quo feels familiar and safe even when it's bad for you.
Which is why we come up with all kinds of excuses for our lack of
action rather than admit our fears. But what all these excuses really
do is stop you from doing what could make you very happy.

Games we play to stay in our comfort zones

The "What if..." game:

Our imaginations picture the most terrible scenarios. So we think, better
to do nothing than risk one of these fantasies coming true.

The "I'll ... when ..." game:

The time is never right when you play this game. I'll go back to college
when the children are older, I'll look for another job when I've got more
confidence, I'll finish my bad relationship when I feel stronger, I'll join a
gym when I've lost ten pounds. It's never going to happen!

The "I can't help being a control freak" game:

Control is the biggest fear of all. It's needing to know everything and
everyone will be an exact certain way before you take action. But how
can you *really* know what's best for others?

Fear vs. intuition

Intuition is always gentle, fear is not. When you're stuck on a decision, listen for the inner feeling that things are right—or wrong. Your subconscious mind gives you messages at the most important times, but if you're too busy, or not inclined to listen, you'll miss out on your very own built-in adviser.

Life will guide you if you let it, so sit quietly and ask yourself, "What do I want?". And intuition can work best when your conscious mind is otherwise engaged, which is why some of your best ideas occur when you least expect them. Take the time to daydream, or ask yourself this question last thing at night before you drop off to sleep.

Fear of failure

Fear of not succeeding can stop us taking any action at all. The saying "if you don't try, you can't fail" may be true, but the opposite is even more so. If you don't try, you will *never* get what you want. The way successful people look at failure is this: it's impossible to fail, you just learn a way *not* to do something.

10 reasons to make you fail

You give up too quickly.

You're not prepared to work hard.

You haven't got a clear picture of what you want.

You set an unrealistic time goal.

You have no clear strategy.

You lack commitment to do your very best.

You let mistakes set you back.

You focus on the end result, rather than enjoying the effort it takes to get there.

You have no support system.

You expect to fail.

WHAT IS YOUR INACTION COSTING YOU?

So moving forward may be a risk, but what about the cost of staying put? While you're waiting to make that all-important decision, you're probably feeling bored, frustrated, and disappointed. Chances are, any action will cost you much less.

CURIOSITY vs. FEAR

Children dive straight in because they have a natural curiosity about life. Give yourself permission to be childlike, and get curious. What opportunities are out there? What can you learn? Where can you look? Who can you ask? Look without pressure to perform. There's no commitment to follow anything through. Unless you want to, of course...

Help—I can't make a choice!

But you already have.
By not choosing a way forward, you're choosing to stay put.
And you're also choosing to live a life that's less than it could be.

Fear of change

It's been said that the only person who likes change is a wet baby. Faced with change of any kind, most of us dig our heels in and resist. But by fighting change, you're actually missing out on most of life's opportunities.

COPING WITH CHANGE

Do accept that change happens. No one's life stays the same (and be honest, would you really want it to?), so when change comes along, don't resist it. You can't stop it, but you can make the best of it.

Don't ignore the warning signs. How many times have you been surprised by something you knew was coming? You just chose to ignore it. Stick your head in the sand and change will sneak up on you when you're least ready for it.

Do be open to opportunities. Rather than seeing change as negative, look for the positive possibilities. How can this change benefit you? What can you do to make the most of the situation? How can you be prepared?

Don't drag your feet. It won't stop the change happening, but it will stop you moving with it and coming out on top.

Do enjoy the challenge. When you see change as a chance to learn and grow, life will feel like one big adventure.

Some changes seem so big you feel terrified just thinking about them. But who said you have to do everything all at once? Break the action up into small steps and suddenly it becomes much less alarming. What's the first thing you can do to bring you closer to where you want to be? When you're stuck, doing *anything* will help change your perspective and give you confidence. And you may just find your fears are unfounded.

Fear fieldwork

Take a risk a week. Plan to have at least one new experience that feels a little out of your comfort zone. It doesn't matter whether it's big or small, just as long as you feel great once you've done it. With each action you survive (and maybe even enjoy), you'll raise your self-esteem and lessen your fear of the unknown.

5 ways to make fear work for you

1 Recognize that fear can be useful. It helps protect you from potential harm when you're not sure of the outcome.

2 Remember fear is a sign that something exciting is about to happen, so don't use it as an excuse to turn your back on every opportunity.

3 Analyze what your fear is trying to tell you. Is it reacting to something that happened in the past (to you or someone else), or to the reality of a situation? Get back to the here and now before you make a decision.

4 Decide how you want to use this information. Will it give you an excuse to procrastinate some more, or will it give you the courage to move forward?

5 Taking action despite your fears will boost your self-esteem. A far more positive feeling than punishing yourself for doing nothing.

You may think fear is caused by a specific situation, but it's far more likely to be linked to your state of mind. A first date can be as enjoyable as a visit to the dentist, but it's not the prospect of making small talk for three hours that brings you out in a sweat, it's the possibility of rejection at the end. Giving up your job to write the novel you've always dreamed of is a risk made most scary by your possible loss of face if you don't get published. The solution? We protect ourselves from danger by doing nothing at all.

false evidence

appearing real

Fear is often **f**alse **e**vidence **a**ppearing **r**eal to the frightened person. It kicks in when it recognizes a situation that's similar to one that may have caused you pain in the past. It wants to protect you from having that same feeling again and works to stop you from taking the action. Your job is to assess if there's any real danger or whether this is a risk that could bring good rewards.

FACT: To gain anything, you have to take a risk. You've been taking risks since you took your first steps as a baby. You take a risk every time you change jobs—or hairstyles. How boring would life be if you never did anything new?

Top 5 fearbusters

1 **Do it fast.** The longer you think about it, the bigger it will become in your mind.

2 **Picture yourself doing it.** Close your eyes and visualize yourself doing what you fear. Is it really *that* scary?

3 **Make it easy.** Choose the easiest option first and you'll gain confidence when you complete it.

4 **Give yourself a reward.** Make it big enough to motivate you into action.

5 **Get yourself a partner.** Nothing seems so scary when there's another person to help you through.

Think of a scary situation you're facing right now and write down a list of all your fears. Now go through the list one by one asking yourself the following questions:

What is the threat to my safety that makes me feel this way?
How old do I feel when I experience this fear?
Is the fear real or are these feelings from the past that actually have no relevance to what is happening right now?

Only when you can see your fears clearly for what they are will they start to loosen their grip on your life.

Do the thing you fear, and the death of fear is certain.

RALPH WALDO EMERSON (1803 – 1882)

Giving life **your own meaning**

Things are not always as they seem. In fact, most of the time they're anything but! We give our own meaning to just about everything that happens to us, but this usually has less to do with the reality of the situation and more to do with our habitual way of seeing the world. What meaning are you giving to what happens in your life?

REALITY: Your partner sits in front of the TV all night.
POSSIBLE MEANINGS:
　a) Work is tough and he or she is too exhausted to talk.
　b) Your partner doesn't love you anymore.

REALITY: Your friend hasn't called you for two weeks.
POSSIBLE MEANINGS:
　a) She's rushed off her feet.
　b) She doesn't consider your friendship important.

REALITY: Your boss has promoted someone else.
POSSIBLE MEANINGS:
　a) The successful candidate has more experience than you.
　b) Your boss thinks you're useless at your job.

Think about something that is bothering you right now.

What is the reality of the situation and what meaning are you giving it? ASK YOURSELF: Is this meaning true? Not true inside your head, but really true in the outside world?

Does your partner really not love you anymore?
Does your friend really not value your friendship?
Does your boss really think you're a waste of space?

Probably not. Yet most of your unhappiness comes from believing these things are true. If the meaning you're giving a situation is adding to your stress, drop it and choose another. After all, you've completely invented the first one, so who's to say a more positive meaning won't be more accurate? Remember, things are not what they seem, they are what they *are*.

WHO DOES YOUR INNER VOICE BELONG TO?

Most of us have an inner voice of doom. One that keeps up a running commentary throughout the day (and night). This voice rarely has anything positive to say. Instead it questions your every move, and usually finds you lacking in some way. Our inner conversation is why many of us hate to be alone. And if we are, we'd rather turn the TV on and drown out the negative voice in our head than risk some quiet. In fact, you're probably so used to your own inner voice, you hardly even notice it's there. Or how much it affects your life.

Turn off the TV and sit in silence.

Notice the internal conversation in your head. Who does the voice belong to? Your mother, your father, your teacher, your ex-partner? What does it say about you?

> You'll never find anyone to marry you unless you lose weight.
> You've never been organized, so how can you expect to run a successful business?
> If you were a natural writer you'd have been editor of the school paper.
> You were always a slow learner, so don't go getting ideas above your station.

Just being aware of who's talking can take away the voice's power. And next time you hear it? Stop the voice in mid-sentence and recognize it as someone else's opinion. You don't have to agree with it.

Why does it **always happen to me?**

Playing the victim is a terrifying way to live. As long as you believe bad things always happen to you, you'll never be in charge of your life. But there's a payback for victimhood, which explains why many of us choose to continue living a life that makes us unhappy. Why we stay in bad jobs and bad relationships. Once you understand what you're getting out of your present situation, the reason you stick with it becomes much clearer.

What could you possibly be getting from staying in a job where your boss is rude to you?

POSSIBLE PAYOFFS: All your friends hate their jobs and it gives you something in common to moan about. Every time you relate your boss's latest rude remark you get lots of sympathy.

What could you possibly be getting from being 30 pounds over your desired weight?

POSSIBLE PAYOFFS: If you lost weight, you may have to start doing all the things you promised you'd do: take up t'ai chi, run the marathon, leave your relationship... If you weighed what you've always wanted, you'd have no excuse not to give up your dead-end job and find a better one.

What could you possibly be getting from being unhappy in your career but "not knowing" what you want to do next?

POSSIBLE PAYOFFS: If you knew what you wanted, you'd have to do something about it. If you never take the plunge, you won't have to face your fear of failure.

By remaining a victim, you stay in your comfort zone.

You also have lots to complain about, and we all love to moan. Listen the next time you're out with friends and see how much of the conversation is taken up with complaints. About their partners, their jobs, their parents, their children, their neighbors. Most of us accept complaining as a major part of our interaction with others, but the more you focus on what's wrong in your life, the less you'll notice what's right. And the more you take each setback or slight personally, the more evidence you're collecting to back up your belief that everyone's out to get you.

Watch how many times you complain every day.

What are your most frequent moans?
What are you getting from keeping these problems in your life?
What would you lose if you no longer had these things to complain about?
What would you gain?
Pick a complaint that's so common you've built it up into an ongoing saga, and decide to solve the problem once and for all.

List the payoffs you get from staying stuck in one area of your life. What don't you have to do?
What don't you have to face?
What story do you get to keep about yourself? Being this honest isn't easy, but once you see why you're behaving in a certain way, you can do something about it. And suddenly you're not stuck anymore.

Minor risks:

Put the risk in perspective.

Is this something that will have a serious effect on my life in six months' time?

Major risks:

Be prepared.

Successful people assess the worst-case scenario in any situation and decide if they can cope *before* they take the plunge. If the very worst you can imagine actually happened, what would you do? Could you handle it? Would the sky fall in?

Dependables

No matter what else is going on around you, who and/or what can you fully rely on?

Your family.
Your friends.
Your partner.
Your humor.
Your integrity.
Your energy.
Your compassion.
Your talents.

reducing the risk

What's the **worst** that can happen?

We all have overactive imaginations which visualize the most terrible things, but look at your decision more calmly and the worst is probably not nearly as bad as you think. If you can handle that, then you have absolutely nothing to fear. Asking this question is also a great way of testing your commitment. What are you prepared to give (or give up) to make your dream a reality?

Most of us take ourselves and our decisions far too seriously, but few decisions are life-threatening. If you make the wrong investment, you may lose money. If you move abroad, you can always come back. If you choose the wrong job, you can find another. If you buy the wrong house, a realtor near you will be only too happy to sell it for you. See left to move forward.

What can I do to **protect** myself?

If fear is keeping you stuck, remember that all risk is reducible, and preparation shows a belief in yourself.

RESERVES
Build reserves to reduce the danger before you take action.

Reserves of money.	Reserves of energy.
Reserves of time.	Reserves of love.
Reserves of support.	Reserves of knowledge.
Reserves of determination.	Reserves of space.

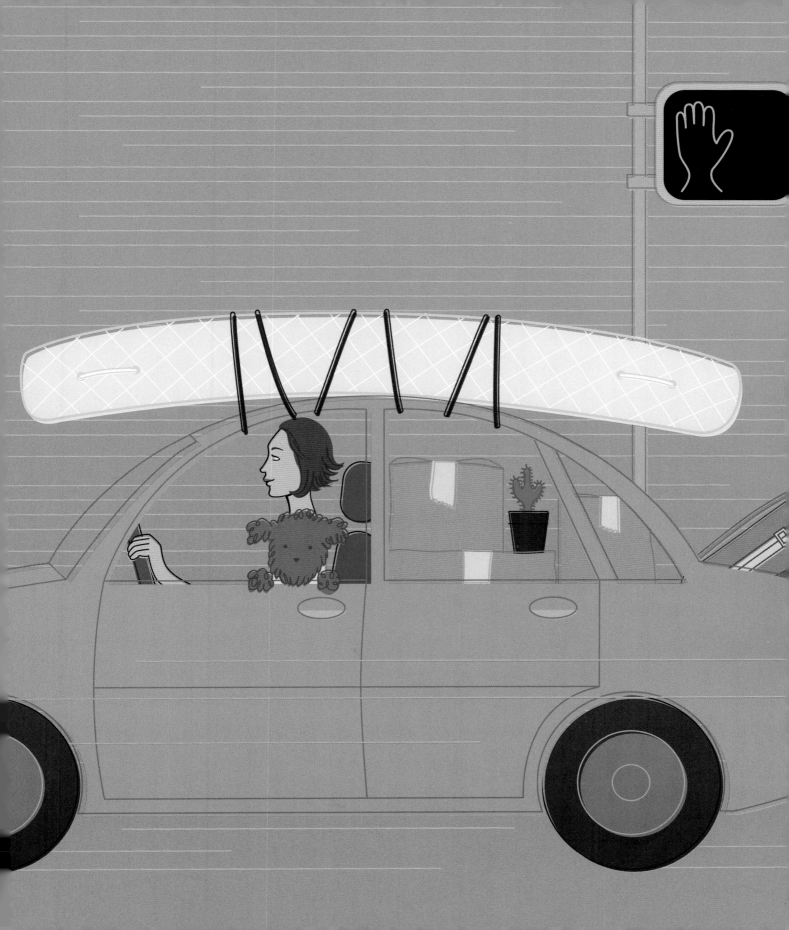

The greatest danger for most of us is not that our aim is too high and we miss it, but that it is too low and we reach it.

MICHELANGELO (1475–1564)

How much money do you need in the bank to feel safe before you take action?

How much free time do you need, in order to do what it takes to make this a success? (See Part 4 for ideas on how to find more time.)

Who do you know who can offer support (emotional or financial) if times get tough? Are they willing to help?

How can you change your lifestyle to maximize the amount of energy you'll need to pull this off?

Who will offer you unconditional love no matter how successful your day has been?

What more do you need to know before you feel confident enough to take action? Who can you learn from?

What room/shelves can you clear to give you the space you need to be totally prepared?

There's no guarantee you'll succeed at everything you do, but sometimes you just have to start. The only way to feel better about doing something is to do it.

do **what it takes**

When you begin to take action, not only does your fear disappear, you also get a big boost to your self-esteem. Sitting around waiting for the right moment will never work. You get excited about something *after* you start doing it, not by thinking about it. And ignorance can be bliss. All you need to know is that you're willing to do whatever it takes to make what you want happen.

One thing *is* guaranteed. Once you take the plunge, you'll create natural energy and motivation as you realize that fear is no longer stopping you from living the life you want. And stay flexible. The fewer rules you have of how things are supposed to be, the more you'll be open to what comes along. And the more you'll enjoy the whole journey.

Your **best** is enough

Success is a combination of hard work and good timing. How much effort are you willing to put into your success? You need to want to take action for the sake of it, not just to reap the rewards. If you hate your 9 to 5 job but stick with it in the hope of getting a raise in April, you might just be disappointed. But if you enjoy what you do, you naturally put in more effort and things start going your way. You get a raise, and a grateful boss. It's a cliché, but the more you put in, the more you get out every time.

Be prepared for a bad day. Don't give up your whole investment in yourself just because it's taking longer than you first expected. Quitting is the number one reason why people fail, yet many quitters use it to protect themselves from failure. When the going gets tough, they get out before anyone can accuse them of failing. So they never put themselves in a position where they could fail—or succeed.

"What good will asking my boss for what I want do?", you ask. What good will not asking do? One way you stand a chance of getting it, the other assures you fail. What have you put off because of fear? Commit to taking action this week. Prepare— and then do it. FACT: No one is free from fear, but some people act despite it.

part 4

Who's in charge
of your life?

What are the obstacles getting in the way
of you living your potential? Remember,
whatever you're willing to put up with
is exactly what you'll have in your life.

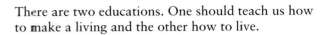
There are two educations. One should teach us how to make a living and the other how to live.

JOHN ADAMS, 2ND US PRESIDENT (1735 – 1826)

what are you
putting up with?

We humans have learned to suffer a lot, most of which isn't necessary. We accept, take on, and get dragged down by other people's behavior and situations, and we're taught not to complain. But it doesn't have to be this way. You're putting up with more than you think and it's draining your energy, causing resentment, and stopping you from living your best possible life.

SOME EXAMPLES OF MINOR AND MAJOR IRRITATIONS

At home

My shower curtain is moldy and smells musty.

My washing machine has been broken for weeks.

My mattress is old and uncomfortable.

My wardrobe is full of clothes I never wear.

My house is littered with magazines and newspapers I never read.

I notice more rust on my car each year.

I live miles away from my friends and family.

My mortgage repayments consume most of my salary.

At work

My desk is a mess and I can't find anything.

I never leave work before 7:30 at night.

My coworkers spend their free time moaning about work.

I suffer backache from sitting in a badly designed chair.

My boss criticizes me in front of others.

I'm paid less than anyone else on my level.

I have no chance of promotion in my current job.

I'm stuck in a profession I no longer enjoy.

Take a few minutes to write down all the things that are currently stressing you out—at home and at work, with friends and family, and in yourself. Don't worry about how you're going to fix them yet. Just put them on paper so you can start to become aware of exactly what's irritating you.

In your relationships

All my friends burden me with their problems.

My partner watches TV in silence every evening.

I have friends who always let me down.

My ex-partner's mother continues to phone me
although I've asked her not to.

My family demands too much of my time.

My sister is very competitive and causes arguments.

I don't have any single friends to socialize with.

My neighbors play loud music late at night.

In yourself

My hair always looks a mess.

I don't have time to relax.

My skin is more broken out now than when I was a teenager.

I spend all my time taking care of others rather than myself.

I never have enough energy.

I'm in debt and scared to look at just how much I owe.

I've put on over 15 pounds in the last year.

I feel dissatisfied with my life but don't know where to
start changing it.

There are two ways to tackle irritations and both
will make you feel more powerful and in charge of your life.

1   You can work out the actions and requests needed to
    eliminate these items from your life. This can often simply
    be a case of telling the truth.

2   You can accept the reality of the situation, let go of
    trying to control it (or them), and focus on something
    far more rewarding. FACT: When we fight life, we
    nearly always lose.

The more you recognize
and deal with the things
you don't like in your life, the
easier it will get. Start with the
small things that are irritating
you and work up to the more
important issues. Once you
see what's possible, you'll
have enough confidence to
face the big stuff.

Symptom vs. source

Don't just focus on the symptom. You must handle the source of the problem or it'll keep coming back to haunt you. For example, if you're in debt, you need to visit a financial adviser who'll be able to tell you the best way to consolidate your finances and start to pay the debt off. But it's just as important to take a look at why your spending went way over budget. Where did the money go, and what have you got to show for it? Why did you feel the need to spend more than you earn? Imagine you had to cut your spending by 25 percent. What would have to go? This may involve changing your lifestyle for a year or cutting up your credit cards, but if the result is a financially secure future with savings to invest in what's really important to you, won't it be worth it?

Begin to ask for what you need and want, and that's exactly what you'll get. The more you become responsible for your life, the more people you'll attract who want to treat you as well as you treat yourself.

Eliminate one minor irritation this week, and one major one in the next 28 days. Once you see how good this feels, commit to working through your list until every irritant is out of your life for good.

How you could handle some of the previous irritations

MINOR IRRITATIONS

You can buy a new shower curtain and brighten your bathroom.

You can go through your closet and give away all the clothes that don't make you feel good.

You can start doing things you enjoy at lunchtime rather than listening to your moaning colleagues.

You can ask your partner to eat dinner at the table each night instead of on the sofa in front of the TV.

You can visit a couple of local salons for a free consultation to find a hairdresser you trust.

You can cut in half the number of newspapers you have delivered —and the bill.

You can visit a dermatologist for expert skin advice.

You can book your car into the bodywork shop for urgent rust removal before it gets worse.

You can write a letter to your ex-partner's mother explaining how painful it is to remain in contact.

MAJOR IRRITATIONS

You can visit a mortgage adviser to discuss changing your lender.

You can read the relevant job pages and sign up with a recruitment agency.

You can upgrade your circle of friends to include more positive people.

You can eat natural foods to boost your energy levels.

You can choose a halfway rendezvous point to meet up with your friends and family regularly.

You can delegate work so you leave the office at 6 p.m.

You can research your dream career on the Internet.

You can ask work to provide a back-friendly chair—or bring in your own.

You can start making decisions based entirely on improving your quality of life.

Now, what can you do about the things in your life that are making you suffer?

10 benefits of being irritant-free

You get more done.

You suffer less stress.

You're surrounded by more positive people.

You stop wasting time worrying.

You have more energy.

You feel more powerful.

You stop being a victim.

You feel in control.

You have higher standards.

You enjoy a better quality of life.

where are you
wasting your time?

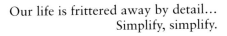

Never have enough hours in the day? You'd be surprised by how much extra work you create for yourself. How much time do you waste on things that aren't necessary? Or because you can't find something? Or doing stuff because you think you should? The result is you end up spending most of your time on things that don't really matter to you and not enough time on what's truly important.

10 ways to uncomplicate your life

PERSONAL

1 **We spend an average of one hour a week paying bills.** Use just one to set up direct debits and remember you now owe yourself an extra hour of pleasure a week.

2 **If it doesn't feel right, say no.** How often have you been stuck with a task, which you knew at the time you agreed to it, you wouldn't want to do?

3 **The more your space is cluttered,** the more time you'll spend searching for things. Give away stuff you don't need and sort out the rest. Your life will run more smoothly.

4 **We live in a world where we're made to feel guilty for doing nothing,** so we over-schedule our lives and leave no time to relax. Regularly give yourself permission to sit and do nothing more than think—you may be surprised by what comes up.

5 **Shopping can be fun,** but not if every lunchtime's spent rushing to the supermarket or buying a birthday card. Shop on the Internet and buy cards in bulk, or say it with flowers ordered over the phone in five minutes.

Time suppliers

If you regularly have to repeat work, be completely clear what your boss expects of you before you begin.

If you regularly lose your car keys, put a hook by the door and store them there.

If you never have an ironed shirt, take five to the dry-cleaner to be ironed every weekend.

PROFESSIONAL

6 **Know your top priorities.** Start each day with a clear idea of what you want and need to achieve, and only spend your time on activities that move you towards accomplishing those goals.

7 **Haste makes waste.** How many times have you quickly skim-read an e-mail before sending off a reply, only to have to answer a second one because you missed an important point?

8 **Eliminate interruptions and distractions.** Tell coworkers when it's OK to disturb you and when you need to be left alone. Tell friends and family if you're too busy to talk and give them an alternative time when they can have your full concentration.

9 **Plan your calls in advance.** How often do you make a phone call without thinking what you want to say, then have to pick up the phone again because you've forgotten to ask a crucial question?

10 **Fully respond to problems.** A situation only turns into a problem if you ignore it the first (or second) time.

Time stealers

What are your own personal time wasters? Long phone conversations, television, video games, crossword puzzles, Internet surfing, worrying? Write a list of the activities that eat into your time and promise yourself you won't indulge for more than an hour a day. You'll be amazed by how much free time you suddenly have available.

who's taking
advantage of you?

How much of your time is spent doing things you want to do? And how much is wasted doing things just because you were asked? Perhaps it's time to drop your disease to please and raise your boundaries. After all, haven't you got better things to do than other people's business?

Boundaries are imaginary protective lines you draw around yourself to stop people from doing certain things to you. Your boss asking you to work late to correct someone else's mistake. Your sister presuming you'll babysit at a moment's notice. Your partner expecting a lift home every time he or she misses the train. Your mother making promises on your behalf without consulting you first.

Most people don't mean to upset or annoy you, but the lower your boundaries, the more you'll attract people who think it's OK to want something from you. The result? You spend time getting annoyed with others when the person you're really mad at is yourself for saying yes.

Ways people take advantage of you

1 **Not taking no for an answer.** Asking for help after you've already said it doesn't suit you. Pushing for personal information when you're obviously uncomfortable giving it.

2 **Pushing you further than you want to go.** Asking for more after you've already done what was originally asked. Persistently asking when you've made it clear you don't want to do something.

3 **Not respecting your personal possessions.** Invading your personal space—looking in drawers, in your bag, at your e-mails. Asking to borrow items and then never returning them or returning them damaged. Using your things without asking—making a phone call, making a sandwich, running an errand in your car.

4 **Ignoring what you want.** Insisting you stay for another drink when you've made it clear you want to go home. Carrying on a conversation when you're obviously busy or trying to concentrate on something else.

5 **Not respecting your time.** Offering your help to others without first checking with you. Regularly canceling arrangements at the last minute or keeping you waiting.

Many people who take advantage have no idea they're doing anything wrong, because you've never given them any reason to think their behavior is unacceptable. Maybe you've never even thought this way before—you just wondered why you felt irritated by certain people or situations. But this is nearly always a sign that your boundaries are weak, and the only way you can avoid this feeling is to do some construction work.

Think of boundaries as personal rules that keep you protected from people and situations that make you uncomfortable or angry. When you've raised yours, not only will your anxiety disappear, you'll also feel more in control of your life. You're simply showing how much you value yourself.

At first it may feel strange being so direct, but once you get more skilled at boundary building you'll automatically deal with unacceptable behavior before it becomes a problem. Remember, people only treat you the way you've educated them to. All they need is a little re-educating on what's acceptable to you—and what you're no longer willing to put up with.

How to teach others to **treat you right**

1 **How can anyone know** you feel irritated, angry, or upset unless you tell them? The first step is simply to inform the other person that this is how you feel. Three golden rules that ensure a positive response:

❋ Keep your voice calm and uncritical. The minute you get emotional, you've lost control of the situation. If you think this is going to be difficult, practice alone before you confront the other person.

❋ Use "I" statements so the words you speak are all about how *you* feel or think. That way no one can argue that you're wrong—all you're doing is explaining what's going on in your own head. "I feel ... when ... happens," will get you so much further than an all-out attack such as "You're so selfish when you ..." Using "you" statements just gets the other person on the defensive, and before you know it, you're in an argument with no chance of getting what you want.

❋ Look and sound confident that you'll get what you want. Don't mumble, stare at the floor, or bite your nails. You deserve to be treated well, so don't be shy about conveying this message to others.

2 **The next step is to inform the other person** what new behavior you would like from them. Now they know that the old style isn't working for you, tell them what will. "I would be very grateful if you would ... from now on," is hard to refuse.

Start by practicing on people you're confident won't offer much resistance, and work up to the more tricky people and situations when you feel more comfortable asking for what you want. Unfortunately, there'll always be people who like to push it (think of how children keep testing what they can get away with!), so you need a backup plan for more difficult encounters.

3 **Let the other person know what will happen** if they continue to ignore your request.

If you continue to put me down, I won't be able to visit you any more.
If you continue to raise your voice, I'll have to leave the restaurant.
If you continue to criticize my driving, I'll not be able to pick you up again.

Only you can decide what your next action will be, but once you inform the other person, you must carry out your intention or they'll never respect your request. You may choose to leave the room, leave the house, and ultimately leave the relationship if the other person continues the actions that upset you.

DON'T TAKE IT PERSONALLY

You can only be responsible for the words that come out of your own mouth. How the other person answers will depend on their own thoughts and feelings, not yours, so don't take their reaction personally.

Who is currently taking advantage of you? Make a list of the people and situations that are upsetting you and decide to tackle one a week with this three-step plan.

1　Tell them what it is you don't like.
2　Tell them what it is you would like.
3　Tell them what you are prepared to do if they continue with the behavior that upsets you.

Just say no

Next time you're asked to do something you don't want to do, speak up. The more you say no to the things you don't want, the more you can say yes to the stuff you do.

6 polite ways to say no

❈ If you'd let me know earlier, it may have been OK, but I'm afraid it's not now.

❈ Please don't ask me to do this again, as I'll always have to say no.

❈ I'm sorry, but tonight isn't possible for me.

❈ I can see something needs doing, but it should be done by the person who caused the problem.

❈ If that's what you want, you're asking the wrong person.

❈ I know I've done this in the past, but I'm afraid it doesn't feel right for me any more.

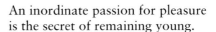

An inordinate passion for pleasure
is the secret of remaining young.

OSCAR WILDE (1854–1900)

whose life
is it anyway?

The **good** "S" word

We're brought up to believe that putting other peop e first makes us good people.
But you can't be fun if you're not having fun. Pleasir g yourself is the only way you're
ever going to please others, and that's where the much misunderstood word *selfish*
comes in. We're taught that being selfish is very bac for the people around us. But if
you're not looking after yourself, how can you even begin to look after others? Listen
to a flight attendant explaining safety precautions. When it comes to the part about
putting on your oxygen mask, the message is very c ear. Adjust your own before
attempting to help others. Why? Because you're going to be no good to anyone
if you haven't first taken care of yourself. Even in far ess perilous circumstances,
chances are you feel uneasy putting yourself first. But if it's good for you, it's almost
always going to be good for those around you.

This month do one thing a week that's unashamedly selfish.

Do it for you because you deserve it. Write a list of things you haven't allowed yourself
to do or to have because they seemed, well, just too selfish. Make the decision that
you're worth it and discover just how great it feels to be *this* good to yourself.

The bad "S" word

Whenever you say the word *should*, you're making a decision based on someone else's agenda. You're also giving away your power. Where are the shoulds in your life?

I should stick with this job and make the best of it.
I should cook my partner a meal every night.
I should visit my parents every weekend.
I should be married by the age of 30.

Make a list of all the things you think you should be doing.

Who is telling you this is right? Who thinks you should stick with a job you dislike? Who said you should be married at a certain age? How long are you going to let your mother, your friends, or the media run your life? Now, replace each should with one of the following:

❊ I could...
❊ I choose...
❊ I decide...
❊ I want...

See how this hands the responsibility back to you?
I could cook my partner a meal every night is now totally your choice.
And if it's not right for you, you can make the choice to drop it.

Daily de-stressers

❃ Practice an attitude of gratitude and remember all the things you have to
be grateful for.

❃ Get up 30 minutes earlier so you have some quiet time in the morning.

❃ Read a book—the concentration needed will transport you from your troubles.

❃ Get out in the fresh air at least once a day and let nature calm you.

❃ Always allow 10 minutes extra travel time so you never arrive uptight.

❃ Eat regular light meals during the day, and never on the run, no matter how
busy you are.

❃ Do something active every day, whether it's walking, yoga, or dancing in
your living room.

❃ Give yourself permission to relax and process the day when you come
home—this will help you leave it behind.

The **price** is right

The house needs cleaning. The car needs washing. You promised you'd walk next
door's dog. You promised you'd run your partner an errand. The next time you feel
pulled in a hundred different directions, ask yourself the following question:
How precious is my time to me?

How much money is an hour of your free time worth to you? $50, $100, $150?
If your time is worth this much, what can you no longer do with it? Who else can
you pay to do the jobs you hate? What do you need to start saying no to?

part 5

Who do you need to be,
to live your potential?

Life gives you what you're ready for.
Are you sending out the right signals?

To love oneself is the beginning
of a lifelong romance.

OSCAR WILDE (1854–1900)

Have you ever noticed how when you feel good about yourself, others feel good about you, too? But the more you tell other people what a failure you are, the more you (and they) will believe it. The moral? If you don't have anything good to say about yourself, don't say anything at all!

image conscious

We choose our self-image, so don't make up your mind too quickly since it will determine exactly what happens in your life. AN EXAMPLE: If you believe you're happy about half the time, when things are going well you'll be waiting for it all to go wrong. And when it does go wrong, you can say you knew the good time wouldn't last. A poor self-image makes you believe you're not worthy of the good stuff, and it won't be long before you're sabotaging any opportunities that come your way.

SELF-ESTEEM vs. SELF-CONFIDENCE

Both are great, of course, but while self-confidence comes from believing in your own competence, self-esteem is far more precious. It's believing in your own self-worth. Self-confidence will help you *do* things more easily, self-esteem will allow you to *be* the best you can be.

SELF-ESTEEM vs. A BIG EGO

Don't confuse the two. People with big egos need to be the center of attention simply because they have to justify themselves to others. They feel unworthy, so they try to convince everyone else of their value. People with high self-esteem are the opposite. They feel proud of themselves, so don't need other people's praise to boost them up.

10 sure signs you have high self-esteem

You **congratulate friends** on their achievements (and mean it).

You'd **rather be happy** than right.

You can **ask for help** easily and offer it just as quickly.

You've **forgiven others** who hurt you in the past.

You've **forgiven yourself** for past mistakes.

You're **not afraid** to say no.

You can easily **admit when you're wrong.**

You enjoy **making others feel good** about themselves.

You're **willing to listen** to a different opinion.

You see the **positive in people.**

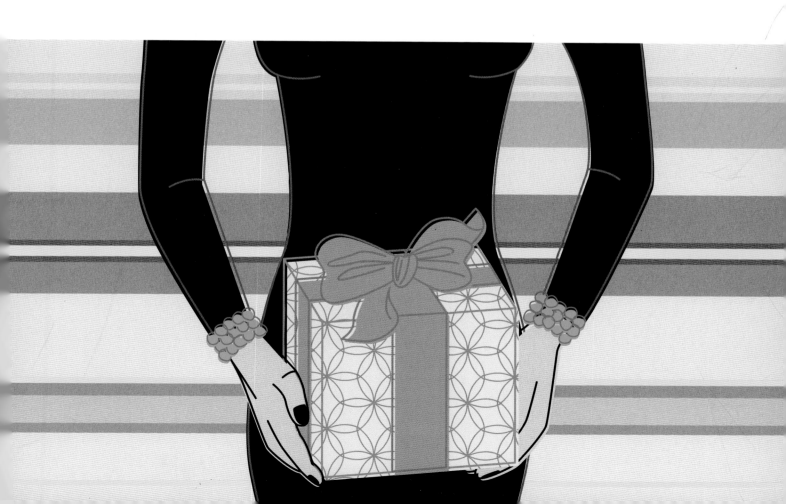

How to **enhance your self-esteem**

What we think about ourselves is based on our experiences, both good and bad.
Unfortunately, we're far more likely to focus on our failures than revel in our successes.

1 When was the last time you felt proud of yourself?

Most of us undermine our own achievements, yet think so highly of others.

Write a list of all the things you're proud of yourself for doing or being.
Begin each sentence with "I'm proud of myself for ... "

I'm proud of myself for passing my exams.
I'm proud of myself for being financially independent.
I'm proud of myself for always telling the truth.
I'm proud of myself for buying a property.
I'm proud of myself for being kind to others.
I'm proud of myself for starting my own business.
I'm proud of myself for looking after the old lady next door.
I'm proud of myself for paying off my credit card debt.
I'm proud of myself for changing career.
I'm proud of myself for giving to charity.

Now that you know which areas of your life make you feel good about yourself,
start to expand on them and acknowledge your actions every step of the way.

2 You can spot someone with a healthy level of self-esteem by the way they accept a compliment. They simply say thank you. They don't need to explain to the other person why they're mistaken ("Oh, this old thing, I've had it for years"), or practice false modesty ("You must be joking, my singing voice is terrible"). They realize how thoughtful it was to offer the compliment—and how rude it would be to throw it back in the other person's face.

Practice saying a simple "thank you" for every compliment you receive, from today onward. It's not egotistical to accept acknowledgment for your achievements, it's good manners.

3 Don't let a successful day, when you accomplished all you set out to do, be ruined by one negative comment. You can encourage a friend in need, speak well in a meeting, and nail a deadline. But receive one less-than-glowing remark from a coworker and that's what will occupy your head all the way home. And the more you dwell on it, the bigger the incident will become in your mind. The result? By the time you arrive home, you'll be convinced the whole office is against you.

Buy a notebook and start keeping a log of all your personal victories. Unless you write them down, the good things you did and the positive things people said will pass you by. Either keep your notebook handy to jot down the good stuff as it happens, or keep it by your bed to write up your achievements before you go to sleep. Recording your personal victories doesn't just give your self-esteem a boost every day. When you're going through a tough time, getting out your notebook and rereading all you've achieved is a sure way to remind yourself that life, and most importantly, you, isn't so bad after all.

How to **boost your confidence**

Your level of confidence will affect the outcome of your actions. FACT: If you feel confident in a situation, you're far more likely to succeed. Luckily there are ways of tricking yourself into having more confidence, even if your past tells a different story.

1 **Act as if you're already confident** in a situation and that's exactly what you'll be. The trick is to stay relaxed. Let yourself tense up and you'll come across more cocky than cool. If you were confident, how would you stand? What expression would you have on your face? What would your voice sound like? What would you say? Practice being that way inside and that's how you'll look on the outside, too.

2 **Remember a time you felt supremely confident.** What were you doing? How did you feel? The next time you need a shot of confidence, visualize the situation again in your mind and enjoy the boost it gives you.

3 **You're never going to feel confident** if your head is full of past failures. Reprogram your brain to focus on the positive by taking 30 minutes to run through the past in your mind, scanning for times when you were most successful. Now, edit out the best bits and press your replay button every time you need a confidence shot.

If people knew how hard I worked to achieve my mastery, it wouldn't seem so wonderful after all.

MICHELANGELO (1475–1564)

Your happiness significantly depends on how much you're able to live in the present. Children do this naturally, but as adults we learn the art of time travel, which allows us to worry about past and future while living in the present. No wonder we feel exhausted!

enjoy the journey

How much time do you spend talking or thinking about past events? Or postponing your happiness until some time in the future when everything will be so much better than it is now? When you have more money, a better job, a smaller waist, a bigger house, or an exotic holiday. Obsessing about the future is an escape from the present. It doesn't matter what's happening right now, it will never be good enough if the future always seems brighter. A guaranteed way to live your life feeling permanently dissatisfied.

When life isn't how we like it, we set goals to change things in the future. But what would happen if you put the same effort into appreciating and improving the present? CLUE: You'd get pleasure immediately, versus waiting around in hope.

The present is a gift—that's why it's called the present.

Make a list of ten reasons why the present is too good to ignore.

Can't think of any? You're not the only one. How about...

10 reasons to be cheerful

❋ You have a healthy body.

❋ And a healthy mind.

❋ You have people who love you.

❋ And people you love.

❋ You have a roof over your head.

❋ And enough to eat.

❋ You have choices.

❋ And freedom.

❋ You have a sense of humor.

❋ And a reason to laugh every day.

There's no such thing as a grateful unhappy person. Or an ungrateful happy one. If you spend your time moaning about your life, you're never going to notice what's positive right now. No one says what you have today is what you must have tomorrow, but if you are only interested in the future, you'll always be struggling. And when you get there, who's to say it's going to be as great as it looked from a distance? Instead, make a decision to focus on the present and enjoy what you have today. You may just realize you don't need to change quite so many things after all.

Why live **in the present?**

❋ The only time that really exists is now.
   The rest is either a memory or a goal.

❋ You'll miss your life if you concentrate on the past or the future.

❋ The only control you have in your life is now.
   The past has already happened, and the future hasn't begun yet.

❋ Living in the future reduces the present to merely a means to an end.

❋ When you expect situations, people, or places to make you happy in the future, you'll be disappointed if they don't live up to your dreams.

❋ Worry and anxiety are nearly always about something that's *already* happened or *might* happen, not about something that is happening right now.

❋ Being impatient for things to happen in the future is a way of punishing yourself for not having made them happen already.

❋ No action can be taken in the past or future.
   To make choices you have to be in the present.

❋ How can you ever feel happy if you spend your life being *here* while wanting to be *there*?

How to practice living in the present

1 See how much more satisfying living in the present feels by giving your whole attention to a routine activity you would normally do without thinking. Smell the flowers on your way to work. Make your evening meal a work of art. How much more can you get out of the mundane chores in your day?

2 When your mind wanders off into the past or future, gently bring it back to whatever's happening right now. What can you do to improve your life this minute?

3 Pay close attention to your thoughts for the next 24 hours. What percentage is focused on the past or future? How much time are you spending in the present? What is keeping you from being there more often?

4 Instead of setting all your goals in the future, word some in the present tense as if they've already happened. Guess what? They will. See below for some examples.

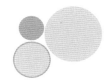

I eat healthy food vs. I will drop a dress size by summer.

I take pride in my work vs. I will ask for a raise next year.

I look after myself vs. I will stop smoking for Lent.

I enjoy my life every day vs. I'll be so much happier when I'm on vacation.

I value my free time vs. I will stop working overtime once I've got a promotion.

who do you need to be, to live your potential?

✳ step three

When people will not weed their own minds, they are apt to be overrun with nettles.

HORACE WALPOLE (1717–1797)

the power of your perspective

Imagination is like a muscle: you must use it or you'll lose it.
The more you develop your imagination, the more you can see what's possible.
Everything starts in the imagination, and by mentally rehearsing an outcome,
you can significantly improve your chances of success (this is why professional
athletes visualize themselves winning before taking part in a race).

Positive thinking may not guarantee success, but it gives you a far better
chance. Picturing yourself first past the finish line won't win you the race if you
haven't put in the training, but imagine yourself coming up the rear and that's
exactly what you'll do. People who lose in life have already pictured themselves
doing so. They see the difficulty in every situation and decide it's impossible
before they've even given themselves a chance of success.

Thinking positive takes practice. Your subconscious mind is made up of your
most *common* thoughts, so one day of good vibes won't be enough to turn your
life around. You've been concentrating on the negative for so long that your
head has lots of proof to back up your worst fears. But start collecting new
evidence today, and your life will begin to mirror what's going on in your mind.

How to create your own reality

GOOD VIBRATIONS

Setting your intention to succeed is like setting the temperature of an oven. Turn up the heat and you start cooking. ASK YOURSELF: What will my life look like when I have ... ? Take 15 minutes to visualize exactly what you want to happen. The clearer the picture in your mind, the stronger your pull toward the outcome you desire.

BAD VIBRATIONS

There's only one way to improve the bad stuff in your life, and that's to stop thinking about it all the time. The more energy you give it, the bigger it will grow.

    If you decide you don't like your mother-in-law, nothing she does will change your mind.

    If you decide you can't trust your partner, nothing he or she does will change your mind.

Check in regularly and examine your thoughts. Are you concentrating on your
mother-in-law/partner's faults and not leaving room for potential new information to change your mind? Change your perspective by indulging in a little people appreciation. Flood your brain with positive thoughts about them and you'll be the one who benefits. FACT: It feels better to love the people we have close contact with, even if we don't understand or approve of everything they do.

If you focus on what's missing, you'll never see what's there. What's working in your relationships right now? How can you expand on the good things so that the negative stuff becomes less important?

Everyone can teach you something about your own life. The next time someone annoys or upsets you, ask yourself this question: What can I learn from you and from this situation?

* A coworker is promoted ahead of you.
  What can you learn from your coworker to improve your own chances of promotion next time?

* A friend has so much more free time than you.
  What can you learn from your friend about putting yourself first?

* Your partner spends hours practicing the guitar.
  What can you learn from your partner about spending your free time doing what you love?

Negative words make you mentally weak and produce bad energy, so be aware of what's coming out of your mouth.

Watch your **language**

The word **try** shows no commitment.
If you were meeting your friend for lunch and she said she'd try and come, would you make the effort to travel an hour to the restaurant? Of course not. When you use the word try, you're not giving your full effort, but substitute *will* for try and you're suddenly in control.

Watch when you use the word **but.**
This is always followed by a negative that often cancels out the positive statement before it. Substitute the word *and* for a far more positive second half to your sentences. Compare "I need to pass this exam, but it's going to be hard work" with "I need to pass this exam, and it's going to be hard work." Which one sounds like you're going to give it your best shot?

Asking yourself **why** questions
just encourages you to obsess about the problem. "Why aren't I better at studying?" won't get you anywhere nearer passing that exam. "*What* can I do to improve my studying?" opens up a possible solution to the problem.

If you believe you **can't,** then that's exactly what will happen.
"I can't study for this exam because I haven't got the free time" will keep you stuck. What you really mean is you *won't*, since you've already decided you're not prepared to put in the effort. "I *could* study for this exam if I gave up my Saturday shopping trip/surfing the 'net/four hours of TV a night habit" shows you're willing to make the compromises needed to succeed. The next time you want to use the word can't, substitute the word *could* and suddenly you're back in charge.

The law of attraction

Like attracts like, which is why when you're looking for new friends or a partner, the best way to ensure the right people come along is to *be* like the person you want to attract. How? Humans are made up of energy, and the frequency of our individual energy flow depends on our feelings. This explains why people who think life gives them nothing get exactly what they expect. It's no coincidence. They're sending out negative energy and attracting more of it back. But people who are positive and open to life's opportunities live far more favorable lives.

Life gives us what we're ready for, so send out the signal that you're ready for action. Concentrating on what you *don't* want will never get you what you *do* want. When you focus on what you don't like about your life, your negative energy expands, ensuring more of the same will be coming your way very soon. But when you focus on what you want, your positive vibes will help bring it to your door. Imagine you're a walking magnet, pulling back everything from the world that matches your energy, and you can you see why it's vital to train your brain to think positively.

Picture something you really want and hold that thought until you start to get excited about how your life will look when you have it.

A great relationship.

A satisfying job.

Optimum health.

If the excitement's not there, it means you're focusing on *not* having the thing you want.

How you've been single for two years.

How you hate the job you have right now.

How you pick up every cough and cold.

Shift your focus to how you'll feel once you reach your goal, and feel the difference in energy.

❋ You like yourself.

❋ You like other people.

❋ You're open to life's possibilities.

❋ You look after yourself.

❋ You enjoy giving without necessarily getting.

❋ You don't complain (much).

❋ You don't worry what other people think.

❋ You live each day as it comes.

❋ You tell the truth.

❋ You don't need much from others.

Now, when do you like **yourself** the most?

Write a list of the times when you're the most likeable and least likeable to yourself.

I'm most likeable to myself when:

I give myself attention.

I compliment others.

I am not affected by others' opinions.

I eat and drink healthily.

I please myself.

I save money each month.

I stay in my own life.

I tell the truth.

How can you maximize your own best behaviors
so you like yourself 100 percent of the time?

I'm least likeable to myself when:

I crave attention.

I criticize others.

I take things personally.

I drink too much.

I try to please everyone.

I overspend.

I attempt to control others.

I tell a lie.

How can you let go or give up your own destructive
and/or restrictive behaviors?

who do you need to be, to live your potential?

step four

be **problem-free**

> If thou art pained by any external thing, it is not this that disturbs thee, but thy own judgment about it.
>
> MARCUS AURELIUS (121–180)

Most of us come up against similar problems over and over again, a sure sign we didn't listen to what life was telling us the first time. But learn to see problems as immediate opportunities and you'll start to love your mistakes. Because without them, you would never learn anything new.

Your quality of life is based 10 percent on what happens to you and 90 percent on how you respond to what comes your way. Facing minor problems before they turn into major headaches will save you hours of stress. And don't beat yourself up when you do make a mistake. Blame, guilt, and worry never solved a problem.

Over-respond so it **never happens again**

Being problem-free doesn't mean never having another problem again. It means facing each new one as it comes along and solving it once and for all. We spend more energy fighting a problem ("it's not my fault/it's not that bad/it wasn't me!"), than we would ever need to solve it. Instead, look for the lesson in each problem and over-respond so it never happens to you again. This means taking at least two actions that tackle the source of the situation. AN EXAMPLE: You frequently scratch your car while parking. Two actions would be to take a refresher driving lesson and practice parking, away from other cars. A further, final action would be to trade your family-sized car in for a smaller, easier-to-maneuver model.

Make a list of the recurring problems in your life that waste your time and energy, and devise at least two actions for each problem that will eliminate it forever.

And one last thing. Let other people solve their own problems. It's not your business, and certainly not in your best interest, to spend your time fixing other people's lives when you could be concentrating on your own.

The reframe game

Have you ever noticed how some people seem to bounce back from problems in their lives? They have exactly the same choices as you, and they choose to reframe the situation into something far more positive. If you don't like the view through your usual glasses, decide to put on another pair and see the world differently. Any successful person will happily tell you how many times they failed before they reached their goal. What makes these people successful is their attitude. They don't see a setback as a failure, but as one step closer to their final success.

> What a problem vs. What an opportunity.
> Life's a struggle vs. Life's a challenge.
> I've made a terrible mistake vs. I've learned a valuable lesson.
> Life's so hard vs. Life's an adventure.

Think of a situation that's making you miserable. How can you reframe it to see a more positive side? There is one, you just have to look for it.

You've lost a contract. Great.
This is just the motivation you need to get out there and find a more lucrative one.

You didn't get the job. Probably a blessing in disguise.
The travel time would have killed your social life.

You've lost a house. Just as well.
The mortgage would have left you no money to enjoy the rest of your life.

Even having a cold can be fun. When else do you have an excuse to
stay in bed and treat yourself to whatever makes you feel better?

HELPFUL HABITS FOR TOUGH TIMES

❋ Now is the time to indulge yourself. We usually treat ourselves when life is good, but you need a massage/a creamy hot chocolate/a day off much more when you're feeling down.

❋ It's easy to have a sense of humor failure when things aren't going your way, but when you lighten up, so does everyone else around you.

❋ Who are the most positive people in your life? Spend as much time as possible with them and let their energy rub off on you.

❋ Forget that never-ending to-do list. What you need is a *done* list to remind you of how much you've achieved, even if you haven't yet reached your final goal.

Who cares **what other people think?**

As long as you hold other people's opinions as important, you will always be a prisoner. Now that you know that humans give their own meaning to every situation, you can see how other people's judgment says more about them than it ever could about you. Understand what's beneath someone's reaction and you can depersonalize their behavior—because it's no longer about *you*.

When you're worried about other people's opinions, you're letting it be about your thoughts, not their actions. Do you really need your parents to be proud of you in order for you to be proud of yourself? Do you really need your friends to approve in order for you to change careers/go traveling/get married (or divorced)? Don't look outside yourself to get what only you can give.

SET YOUR STANDARDS

Choose to raise your standards and you free yourself from ever having to worry about someone else's opinion of you or your actions again. Living with high standards means never doing anything you feel ashamed of yourself for. It means doing things because you want to and because it feels *right* for you. When you're pleased with an action you took or a decision you made, you're almost certainly living up to your best standards. How high are yours? Think back over the last week. Did all your actions make you feel good? Would you be happy admitting them to your friends? Or are you slightly ashamed of yourself?

Remember at all times that other people's judgment is mcre about them than it is about you.

What kind of person do you want to be?
Someone who is kind to others? Who doesn't gossip behind other people's backs? Who always tells the truth? Write out a list of the standards you want to live by and stick to them. You will feel *very* good about yourself.

part 6

What will it take
to get there?

People succeed because they know where
they're going. Isn't it time you had a plan?

what motivates you?

Inertia is the hardest condition to overcome. Think of yourself as being like a car. It takes more energy to start you up than it does for you to cruise down the road. There are two ways to get you motivated: pleasure and pain. You may think the majority of us are motivated by how great our lives will be once we've made a positive change, but often pain works as a far more powerful push. Everyone is different and the secret to breaking out of your inertia is recognizing exactly what motivates *you*.

Pleasure or pain?

You decide to decorate your living room after months of lethargy. What finally motivates you into action? The picture in your mind of how great the room will look once it's decorated? Or the fact that you can't bear to live with such a mess one minute longer?

Major pleasure motivators

Can you recognize what motivates you?

Adventure	Innovation	Support
Results	Accountability	Respect
Creation	Justice	Profit
Responsibility	Visual images	Sharing
Winning	Loyalty	Love
Compassion	Conviction	Encouragement

Write down the motivators that have worked for you in the past and then brainstorm how you can utilize them again to reach your potential.

For example, imagine you've always wanted to start your own business. Here's how you could use the following motivators:

Visual images: design your business card or brochure and put it on the wall by your computer for constant inspiration.

Respect: imagine how impressed your friends and family will be when you've built a successful business.

Profit: draw up a financial business plan and visualize how your increased earnings will improve your quality of life.

Conviction: choose a product or service you're passionate about and your customers will be drawn to you.

Accountability: commit to taking one action a day towards starting your business and ask a friend to check in with you for a weekly update.

Top 10 motivational enemies

Poor self-image	Negative past experiences
Feeling overwhelmed	Low energy levels
Lack of time or money	Limiting beliefs
Unsupportive environment	Other people's judgment
Procrastination	Perfectionism

How can you reduce the demotivators in your life?
What changes do you have to make? What old scripts must you rewrite?

The value of life does not lie in the number
of years but in the use you make of them.

MICHEL DE MONTAIGNE (1533–1592)

How low are you prepared to go?

What if nothing is tempting enough to break your inertia? Instead of focusing
on your rosy future, take a look at how bad things could get if you stay
exactly where you are.

Major pain motivators

Boredom	Anger	Resentment
Frustration	Unhappiness	Loneliness
Bitterness	Dissatisfaction	Disappointment

How does it feel to think you'll still be in the same situation a year from now?
What will your life be like?
How miserable will you be?

Let yourself really feel the consequences of your inaction.
What will it cost you? Now turn it around. What are the benefits of action?

Compare the two outcomes and ASK YOURSELF:
How much longer am I prepared to live a lesser life?

If you're still unsure what motivates you, ask your friends or family to help.
You may be surprised by how much they know about your motives.

step two

the power of positive statements

Even more important than *having* the right things is *thinking* the right things.
The only place where permanent changes take place is in your subconscious
mind. Learn to reach yours and you can begin to set up what you want to
happen in your life. When you focus on what you really want and take regular
actions toward that goal, you can achieve more than you ever thought possible.

Changing your mind, step by step:

1 Sit and think about an outcome you would like in your life. Take ten minutes to really visualize it and why you want it.

2 Write down a positive statement in the present tense that will lead you to what you want to happen.

I'm active every day and my body looks great.

My life is too precious to do work I don't enjoy.

I can handle anything so I have no reason to fear the future.

I value my time, so I only say yes when I want to.

I eat for energy and feel amazing.

3 Memorize this statement word for word and repeat it aloud and in your head many times a day. Positive thinking needs daily practice to cancel out all the negative self-talk. Only when you can repeat it without a pause do you know the statement's reached your subconscious mind.

4 What actions can you take to support what you want to happen?

Do something active every day even if it's just a walk in the park.

Research the extra qualifications you need for your dream job and downsize your spending by 25 percent to pay for retraining.

Write a list of all the times you've survived a difficult situation in the past.

Practice saying no by refusing one request made of you every day.

Eat only fresh, unrefined food for a week.

5 Keep a journal of every action you take that supports your positive statement, and after a month you'll have all the evidence you need to prove this new way of thinking is working for you.

6 Act as if your perfect outcome has already arrived and congratulate yourself on making it happen.

Ten thousand difficulties
do not make one doubt.

CARDINAL NEWMAN (1801–1890)

step three

secrets of success

1 Do it the easy way

We often focus on what we should be doing rather than what comes easily to us.
Life can be difficult enough without ignoring our strengths, so ask yourself what
the simplest solution could be.

 What is the easiest route from A to B? Which choices feel lighter?
Go with these.

2 What do you know already?

We think so little of ourselves we forget exactly how much we already know.
Do you really need to go on another weekend presentation course? Is another
fiction-writing class really necessary? Instead of looking outside yourself for more
knowledge, fully use what you already have.

 What knowledge do you have already that can move you forward today?

3 Narrow your focus

What you focus on expands, so make sure your focus is on exactly what you want. Concentrate on just one thing and all other distractions fall away, so make your goal a priority and do what it takes to move you closer.

 When was the last time you really focused on achieving something? What was the result of your single focus? Are you willing to commit to this kind of attention again?

4 Who can help?

Who do you know who can offer advice or suggest someone else who can? Offer to take them out for lunch so you not only get their full attention for an hour, you get to show your appreciation, too.

 What resources are right under your nose? Who do you know who's done what you'd like to do, in a way you'd like to do it?

5 Create a supportive environment

Don't underestimate how much your environment affects you. Negativity is contagious. After a lunchtime spent with coworkers complaining about pay, would you return to your desk motivated for an afternoon's work? The people you choose to be around right now are a good indicator of how you feel about your life. So if you're planning improvements, you may need to start mixing with a more supportive crowd. People who see the possibilities in life, not the problems. Who encourage you to take action, not warn you of the risks.

 Think about the people you spend the most time with. Do they support you or hold you back? Who are the most motivating people you know? Get back in touch and tell them why you enjoy their company so much. Set up a support system (lunch once a month/a debrief phone call once a week/an encouraging e-mail once a day) and give as good as you get.

6 Start the day as you mean to go on

What start to your day guarantees a good one? From the minute your alarm clock rings, it's up to you how your day unfolds.

a) Do you stay under the covers hitting the snooze button until the last minute, and then drag yourself out of bed and get dressed in the dark? And do you then leave the house feeling tired and grumpy?

b) Or do you lie in bed thinking about the pleasurable things you're going to sneak into your day, and then play your favorite music while you get dressed? And do you then make time for an energy-boosting breakfast?

What are the morning activities that usually mean you're going to have a good day?

Essential oils in your shower.

Your clothes ironed and laid out.

A fresh fruit smoothie.

Breakfast at the table.

Fresh bread or toast.

Wearing gorgeous underwear.

A swim before work.

Playing your favorite CD.

Walking through the park to work.

If your morning routine is always rushed, commit to getting out of bed 30 minutes earlier. Another half-hour in bed makes no difference, but extra time spent getting ready can affect your whole day. And give yourself something to look forward to, so no matter how challenging the day, you can always find one reason to get out of bed each morning.

7 Be open to your possibilities

Have you any idea how severely you limit what's possible in your life by making assumptions? You do it every day.

I'm far too old to go back to college.

They'll have so many applicants I won't even get an interview.

There's no chance of promotion in my company.

I don't have a degree so I won't be qualified enough.

They're far too busy to collaborate with me.

Sometimes we use assumptions to keep us stuck ("what's the point in trying?"), and sometimes we're not even aware we're making them. The next time you start putting blocks in your own way, ask yourself whether this assumption is based on fact. Do you really know it's true? Have you asked? What *could* happen instead?

You may find there are three people older than you in your class.

You may get an interview next week.

Your boss may know of opportunities in the company you aren't aware of.

Your ten years' experience may count for much more than your lack of a degree.

Your chosen business partner may have been busy six months ago but is now looking for a new project.

To make changes in your life, you have to start believing that anything is possible. And don't let yourself be crushed by a single negative response. One lecturer may express concern over your age, but that's only their opinion. And that opinion is based on their own experience (or lack of it). Rather than take it personally, see how another person's view is merely their take on the world, and one that possibly protects them. Maybe this lecturer would rather believe 35 is too late to retrain than admit the possibility that they could be following their own dream.

What assumptions are you making that stop you from living your potential? Are they *the* truth or just your version, or someone else's version of it? What else is possible? How can you find out? List the many choices available to you and start from there.

8 Think big

A surprising fact: one major reason why people fail to reach their goals is because the goals aren't big enough. To achieve more, you have to aim for more (and put up with less). Streamline the rest of your life and you'll move forward with the least resistance.

If I could do anything, what would it be? What must I get rid of to make space for this to happen?

9 Think differently

No matter how you usually do things, chances are there's a better way. Thinking outside your usual confines encourages new possibilities. The next time you hit a dead end, get creative. There's a solution out there—you just haven't thought of it yet.

Are you aware you're following a familiar pattern? Is there another way? Is there an alternative view that's outside your usual way of thinking?

10 Energy drains vs. energy providers

Identify what drains your energy and replace each one with an energy provider.

Negative people - - - Positive people.

Junk food - - - Nourishing food.

Secrets - - - Speaking the truth.

Problems - - - Facing each one immediately.

Martyrdom - - - Saying no.

Manipulation - - - Honesty.

Self-sacrifice - - - Putting yourself first.

11 Acknowledge the bad times

When times get tough, you need to have faith in yourself and in your ability to succeed. *But* you also need to be able to face the difficult facts of reality. If you bury your head in the sand and wait for the bad stuff to go away, you're in for an unpleasant surprise. Problems need to be faced and responded to, or they'll sabotage all your good work. Pick yourself up and carry on as many times as you need to. You're doing your best and that's good enough.

12 And remember the good times

At any moment there's something good going on in your life. Stop for a minute
and think about what gives you joy:

Your loving partner.

Your supportive friends.

Your devoted dog.

Your beautiful children.

Your immaculate garden.

Maybe life's not so terrible after all?

step four

planning your progress

Make a success **shopping list**

The reason people with goals succeed is because they know where they're going. You wouldn't go shopping without a list and expect to come back with what you want, so why expect life to work out perfectly without a plan?

10 goals to reach in the next 90 days

Goals give you a clear idea of what you want in life. Writing yours down makes them seem more real and will significantly increase your chances of achieving them. What do you most want to accomplish in the next 90 days? Choose goals you really want to achieve and are ready to have now, not things you should, could, or might want later. What ten goals would really improve your life *right now*?

1 _____

2 _____

3 _____

4 _____

5 _____

6 _____

7 _____

8 _____

9 _____

10 _____

Do choose goals that make you feel excited and a bit nervous. That's what will motivate you.

Don't choose goals that you've failed at in the past unless you're in a much better position to succeed now.

Do surround yourself with like-minded people. So much that happens to you is determined by the people you see or speak to every day, so choose them carefully.

Don't make your goals too vague ("I want to be happier, richer, more successful"). You need to know exactly what you want in order to stand a good chance of getting it.

Do enjoy the doing part, knowing you're moving toward your goal every time you take an action.

Don't share your goals with anyone else unless you know they'll encourage you. And remember, any negative reactions are more to do with the other person's insecurity and dissatisfaction than with your chances of success.

If you could only achieve one goal from your list, which would it be? Start working towards your number one goal today.

Nothing great has ever been accomplished without enthusiasm.

RALPH WALDO EMERSON
(1803–1882)

Your 90-day **progress chart**

✳ Turn an 8½ x 11-inch piece of paper lengthwise
and draw lines to divide it (see right).

✳ Along the top write 1–12 for the weeks,
and in the left-hand column, write a
description of each of your goals.

✳ Put it somewhere you'll see it every day (on
your fridge door/bedroom wall) and commit
to taking one action a week to support each
goal. Tick the box when you've done this.

GOALS	1	2	3	4	5	6	7	8	9	10	11	12

Plan **your strategy**

Going after a goal without a plan is like going on a trip without a map. Success is a combination of hard work and good timing, but you can maximize your chances of success by planning a strategy that shows how you're going to achieve your goal in the smartest possible way. This is your game plan, so make the game worth playing. Keep it simple by visualizing your goal and working backwards. And stay flexible. Our ability to adapt makes us the dominant species on the planet, so take advantage of your natural-born skill. Forget how it *should* be and wait to see how it *is*. You won't know if your strategy is working until you're in the middle of it, so be prepared to redesign as you go.

What are you willing to do day by day, week by week, month by month to make this dream a reality? Put the actions on your progress chart and begin today. What are the five things you can do this week to get you off to a great start?

Persistence vs. stubbornness

Persistence takes courage. It means committing yourself to giving a goal all you've got, with what you've got. Most overnight success stories ignore the months or years the person has worked hard to achieve what they set out to do. But persistence is not the same as stubbornness. There's no shame in exploring an opportunity only to find it's not what you want after all. Many people use the risk of taking a wrong direction as an excuse not to take any at all ("What if I choose the wrong goal and it doesn't make me happy?"). But this can only be a good thing. You have just discovered something that isn't right for you, so you can eliminate it from your list and explore something else that may be *exactly* what you're looking for. The ultimate success is not in doing it perfectly the first time, but picking yourself up and doing it differently the next. FACT: If you don't risk taking action, you risk living a lesser life.

Living your best life

Before you can create your ideal life,
you first need to know what it looks like.

what do you **really, really want?**

Ask yourself the following life-changing questions, holding each one
in your head for a few days if the answer doesn't come immediately.
REMEMBER: The only limit is what *you* think you're capable of.

What is your lifelong dream?

What would give you the most joy?

Where do you want to be in five years' time?

What's the dream you've given up on?

How happy are you on a scale of 1–10?
What would it take to get you to 10?

Who do you need to be in order to live your potential?

What would have to change in order for you to
feel completely fulfilled?

How willing are you to do whatever it takes?

If the above questions sound scary, consider this:
Change will always happen. Do you want it to be unintentional or directed by you?

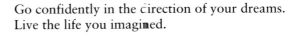
What does your ideal life look like? You need to know in order to be able to create it. Spend a couple of hours designing your ideal life.

design your life

How would you like to experience life on a daily basis?

Where would you live?

What people would surround you?

What work would you do?

What things would you own?

What feelings would you have every day?

Make this your **real** ideal life.

The one you'd live after you'd spent your lottery winnings and gotten bored of lying on a beach every day. Brainstorm for five minutes each day over the next week and put down everything that comes into your head in any order it occurs to you. Keep revisiting your list until you're satisfied you have everything you've ever wanted down on paper.

Use the gap between what you have now and what you want to have in order to motivate you into action. How much faster can you get there now that you know where you're going?

Your one-year **best life plan**

The 10 priorities in my life this year.
What is *most* important to you? Career, financial, personal, social, pleasure, appearance, spiritual, surroundings, people?

The 10 talents I want to use every day.
What great things about you are not being fully utilized?

The 10 opportunities I have right now.
What possibilities are out there just waiting to be explored?

The 10 pleasurable things I want to do every day.
What would ensure you got some enjoyment from every single day?

The 10 people I most want around me.
Who brings you joy?

The 10 big things I want to do this year.
What new things do you want to do—just for you? An adventure, a new skill, an exciting sport, travel?

The 10 standards I want to live up to.
What will ensure you feel good about yourself every day?

The 10 things I will no longer do this year.
What behaviors hold you back from living your best life?

The 10 visuals that will inspire me.
Cover a pinboard with photographs of the people you love, a picture of your dream house, postcards of places you want to visit, cuttings of how you want your garden to look.

It's not death that man should fear, but he
should fear never beginning to live.

MARCUS AURELIUS (121–180)

the big picture

All successful companies have a clear view of where they're going and how
they're going to get there—and so can you. What is your vision for yourself?
Why are you here? What's worth living for?

Indulge in a little **time travel**

One whole year from now, what would you like to be able to say about yourself?
What would your life be like if you were living your vision?

Answer the following questions:

Where am I?

What am I doing?

Where am I living?

Who am I with?

What am I feeling?

Then repeat the exercise three years from now. What else is possible?

Think about the people you admire. Whose life do you envy the most?

What do you think their life is like? What is it you envy about it most? What personal qualities would you need in order to close the gap between your life and theirs?

Pretend you're a successful company

(or a secret agent) and create your own mission statement
to describe how you will make your vision happen.

Finish this sentence:

My mission is to ... _____

_____

_____

_____

_____

_____

_____

_____

_____

_____

_____

_____

_____

_____

_____

_____

_____

your precious life

The unexamined life is not a life worth living for a human being.

SOCRATES (469–399 B.C.)

Seven happy habits and thoughts

You've only got one life, and it's 100 percent up to you how you live it.

1 **This is your life and no one else's.** Make choices based on what you want, rather than being nudged along by what other people think is best for you. Learn to put yourself first and listen to your intuition. Whenever you say the word *should*, it's nearly always followed by something you don't want to do.

2 **Remember how great you are.** We spend so much time beating ourselves up rather than praising our strengths. The next time you do something you like, don't let it pass you by without acknowledging yourself for a job well done.

3 **Success is what you think it is.** Don't measure yourself against some media-inspired or peer-pressure yardstick. If you believe you're successful, that's what you are. And success is not limited to your work. Good friends, family, finances, and fun all make you just as successful as that top job.

4 **Don't waste your time trying.** Either commit to doing something with enthusiasm or find another goal you want badly enough to put in the effort. Be willing to do whatever it takes, and life will start to give you what you want.

5 **Life is not a dress rehearsal.** If you want something, you have to take steps to get it. Settling for the status quo is not enough when there's a gap between where you are now and where you want to be. And don't think you have to do everything at once. One small step a day will take you nearer to your ideal life.

6 **Know what you want—and love what you have.** It's that simple.

7 **Make quality of life your number one priority.** In the end, how you feel about your life will be determined by what you decided to focus on, not by what actually happened.

Now, what are you
going to do with
what's been valuable
in this book?

index